THE
McCARTHY ERA

MILESTONES
IN AMERICAN HISTORY

MILESTONES
IN
AMERICAN HISTORY

THE
McCARTHY ERA

COMMUNISTS IN AMERICA

ANN MALASPINA

CHELSEA HOUSE
An Infobase Learning Company

The McCarthy Era
Copyright © 2011 by Infobase Learning

Chelsea House
An imprint of Infobase Learning
132 West 31st Street
New York, NY 10001

Library of Congress Cataloging-in-Publication Data

Malaspina, Ann, 1957–
The McCarthy era : Communists in America / by Ann Malaspina.
  p. cm. — (Milestones in American history)
Includes bibliographical references and index.
ISBN 978-1-60413-765-1 (hardcover)
1. Anti-communist movements—United States—History. 2. McCarthy, Joseph,
1908–1957—Influence. 3. Internal security—United States—History—20th century.
4. Communism—United States—History—20th century. 5. Subversive activities—United
States—History—20th century. I. Title. II. Series.

E743.5.M17 2011
973.921092—dc22   2011004458

Chelsea House books are available at special discounts when purchased in bulk
quantities for businesses, associations, institutions, or sales promotions. Please call
our Special Sales Department in New York at (212) 967-8800 or (800) 322-8755.

You can find Chelsea House on the World Wide Web at http://www.infobaselearning.com

Text design by Erik Lindstrom
Cover design by Alicia Post
Composition by Keith Trego
Cover printed by Yurchak Printing, Landisville, Pa.
Book printed and bound by Yurchak Printing, Landisville, Pa.
Date printed: July 2011
Printed in the United States of America

10 9 8 7 6 5 4 3 2 1

This book is printed on acid-free paper.
All links and Web addresses were checked and verified to be correct at the time of
publication. Because of the dynamic nature of the Web, some addresses and links
may have changed since publication and may no longer be valid.

CONTENTS

Playwright
on Trial

"My conscience will not permit me to use the name of another person and bring trouble to him,"[1] declared the playwright Arthur Miller before the House Un-American Activities Committee in June 1956. The congressional committee known as HUAC was charged with uncovering Communists and antigovernment activity. Under questioning, Miller had been asked to identify acquaintances who were Communist sympathizers, but he refused to name names. Four years earlier in 1952, Miller's colleague and friend, the prominent director Elia Kazan, was asked the same question. Kazan decided to comply with the request and gave the names of eight people he knew had been members of the party. He told the committee that his brief stint in the Communist Party during the 1930s had ended after he'd "had enough of their habitual violation of the daily practices of democracy that I had become accustomed . . . I had had a taste of police state living, and I did not like it."[2]

Like many of their colleagues in the entertainment business, Miller and Kazan were ensnared in the web of anti-Communist hysteria that overwhelmed American politics and public debate in the late 1940s and early 1950s. The national wave of paranoia was epitomized and sometimes led by a husky, barrel-chested senator from Wisconsin, Joseph R. McCarthy, who served in the U.S. Senate from 1947 until his death in 1957. McCarthy accused professionals in the State Department of Communist sympathies, organized a full-scale investigation of the U.S. Army, and stirred up a public frenzy that destroyed countless lives and careers. Small wonder that the time is known as the McCarthy era, yet the senator was only a part of the terrifying anti-communist movement that swept the nation. In the shadow of the Cold War, which split the world between democracy and Communism, the public allowed for widespread political repression, fearing that dissent amounted to being un-American—and being un-American could tear apart and threaten national security. Reputations were lost, and careers were destroyed. Blacklists banned teachers from public schools, state employees from their desk jobs, and screenwriters from Hollywood. Televised hearings of alleged Communists alarmed and fascinated the nation. McCarthy, who aroused both anxiety and profound distaste, was one of many powerful people who went after suspected Communists and antigovernment activity. Several U.S. presidents, as well as politicians, newspaper editors, and others, jumped on the anti-Communist bandwagon. Possibly even more influential than McCarthy was J. Edgar Hoover, the longtime Federal Bureau of Investigation (FBI) director, who spent decades compiling secret files on suspected Communists and searching out so-called agitators.

In fact, this tumultuous era of fear about the Red Menace (as Communism was known), real or unproven, began unfolding before McCarthy arrived on Capitol Hill and continued after his death in 1958. Congress began investigating Fascists, Communists, and other people and groups suspected of anti-government activities in the 1930s. In 1940, Congress passed the Smith Act, making it illegal to advocate the overthrow of the government. In the following years, the Department of Justice compiled a list of allegedly subversive organizations, and the FBI under J. Edgar Hoover began investigating hundreds of people for Communist ties. The spread of Communism by the Soviet Union after World War II spawned new fears of threats to democracy. The Cold War had begun, and under the shadow of the Soviet Union's reach into Eastern Europe and its progress in atomic research and nuclear weapons, politicians easily exploited Americans' sense of insecurity. Meanwhile, the Communists in China had won a brutal civil war, and the United States joined South Korea in the war against China-backed North Korea in 1950. Anxiety about the menace of Communism was building. In 1951, Julius and Ethel Rosenberg, a middle-class New York couple with two young sons, were convicted of treason and sentenced to death for passing secrets to the Soviet Union.

Like many whose lives were turned upside down during this time, Arthur Miller and Elia Kazan were both highly successful in their fields. The two men came from the same generation, and they were both raised in immigrant, working-class families. Kazan was born in 1909 to a Greek family living in the Ottoman Empire. They arrived in the United States in 1913, and Kazan's father became a rug merchant in New York City. Kazan was expected to go into the family business; instead he attended the Yale School of Drama in Connecticut. In the early 1930s, Kazan joined the Group Theater in New York, a leftist theater group that had connections with the Communist Party. Between 1934 and 1936, Kazan was a member of the party, but he soon quit. In 1947, he cofounded the Actors Studio, a prominent membership organization for actors, directors,

Bowing to pressure from the House Un-American Activities Committee, director Elia Kazan (*right*) provided the names of colleagues who were members of the Communist Party. His betrayal destroyed his relationship with playwright Arthur Miller (*left*).

and playwrights. Kazan brought two of playwright Tennessee Williams's most famous plays—*A Streetcar Named Desire* and *Cat on a Hot Tin Roof*—to Broadway in 1951 and 1955.

Miller was born in Harlem in 1915 to Polish Jewish immigrant parents. His father owned a ladies' coat manufacturing business, and his mother was a schoolteacher. When the family's business went bankrupt during the Depression, the Millers moved to Brooklyn. After graduating from high school, Miller had to work for several years to save up money to go to the University of Michigan, where he studied journalism and began to write plays. The same year he graduated, in

1938, he won a major theater prize. Miller moved to New York City and joined the Federal Theater Project, part of President Franklin Roosevelt's New Deal, and he worked as a writer. In 1944, Miller's play *The Man Who Had All the Luck* opened on Broadway. His second play on Broadway, *All My Sons*, debuted in 1947 and won the Tony Award for Best Play of the Year.

When Miller's stunning play *Death of a Salesman* opened on Broadway in 1946, he had Elia Kazan to thank for much of the play's tremendous success. Kazan was the director of Miller's play about a traveling salesman at the end of his career and his two sons who are fighting their own battles of morality and conscience. Miller won the Pulitzer Prize in Drama for *Death of a Salesman*, and Kazan shared in the acclaim. But a decade later, the friendship between the two men had fallen apart and they were no longer speaking to each other. Their mutual trust was derailed by the fear, accusations, and betrayals that tore apart American society and ruined so many lives.

The House Un-American Activities Committee began investigating the motion picture industry in Hollywood in 1947. Kazan was called to testify on April 10, 1952. Under pressure from Washington, the Hollywood film studios were encouraging people to testify, in hopes of dispelling the shadow of disloyalty that had been cast on the industry. Those who refused to testify were blacklisted by the studios and unable to work. Kazan told the committee that he was a member of the Communist Party in the 1930s. He also said that he was disillusioned by Communism and had turned against it. Then, as the hearing went on, Kazan was asked to inform on others. He gave the names of eight of his old friends who were also members of the Group Theater, and so were now tarnished by the Communist label. If he hadn't agreed to do so, Kazan knew that he would have lost his standing in Hollywood, where he had begun a successful film career. Instead, his testimony damaged the careers of others, including the actors Morris Carnovsky and Art Smith, and Clifford Odets, a leading playwright.

Miller was also briefly interested in Communism. He had joined the Joint Anti-Fascist Refugee Committee and attended a Marxist study course in a storefront in Brooklyn. Communism during this time in the United States was popular among people who were against Fascism, a repressive system of government led by a dictator that emphasized nationalism and often racism. People involved in the labor movement and interested in workers' rights were also attracted by Communism and its concern for the working class. Miller had experienced economic uncertainty after his father lost his business, and he related to the problems of the poor. In 1946, he attended a few meetings of writers belonging to the Communist Party. He was curious about Marxism, the political philosophy behind Communism. But Miller soon discovered that Marxist writers were required to follow the Community Party line and not their own visions, so he lost his interest in it.

After hearing Kazan's experiences before Congress, Miller was filled with dread. He believed it was not the Communists who were threatening the nation, but the anti-Communists who were stirring up hysteria. Miller decided to write a play inspired by the McCarthy era but based on earlier historical events. In 1953, Miller's play *The Crucible* premiered in New York. The fictional story is about the witch hunts in Salem, Massachusetts, in 1692, where women were falsely accused of being witches, but the themes of unjust persecution and mass hysteria also reflected Miller's own experiences in the 1950s. Looking back on the play years later, Miller said what struck him was not the hunt for witches, but the way people watched the hangings—just like people who watched McCarthy during the 1950s. "We were all behaving differently than we used to; we had drunk from the cup of suspicion of one another; people inevitably were afraid of too close an association with someone who might one day fall afoul of some committee. Even certain words vibrated perilously, words such as *organize, social, militant, movement, capitalism*—it didn't do to be on too familiar terms with such language. We had entered a mysterious pall from which there seemed no exit,"[3] he said.

The Crucible won four Tony Awards, including Best Play and Best Author. Yet the reviews were not all positive, and Miller was shunned both inside and outside the theater world for the political message sent by the play. In 1954, the State Department refused to give Miller a passport to attend a meeting in London. The next year, New York City reneged on a plan to cooperate with Miller on a documentary about juvenile offenders. Then in 1956, Miller was subpoenaed to testify before HUAC about a passport renewal application. He was suspected of being part of a Communist conspiracy to misuse American passports.

In the midst of his testimony, he was married to the glamorous Hollywood actress Marilyn Monroe. Monroe attended the hearings in a New York courtroom. By displaying public support for her husband, Monroe was putting her own career at risk, given the political climate. Miller told them of his past participation in Communist meetings, but he refused to reveal the names of other writers and colleagues. In May 1957, he was found guilty of contempt of Congress. He received a fine of $500 and was sentenced to 30 days in prison. Miller was also blacklisted, meaning that he could not work, and he was not allowed a passport.

Miller appealed the ruling, and on August 7, 1958, his conviction was overturned by the U.S. Court of Appeals. Unlike some whose reputations had been tarnished by the McCarthy era, Miller continued to write, but his career still suffered from the bad publicity. His marriage to Monroe ended. Meanwhile, Kazan's career flourished. He directed film classics, including *Splendor in the Grass* and *East of Eden*. He never apologized for his testimony against others in the film industry, yet the McCarthy era left its mark on his work, too. His famous film *On the Waterfront* (1954), a story of loyalty and betrayal, starred Marlon Brando as a dock worker who informs on a union boss for a murder after falling in love with the murdered man's sister.

Although the two were estranged for a time, Kazan directed Miller's autobiographical play *After the Fall* in 1964. Miller's reputation grew, even after his death in 2005, as a moral voice in American theater. Yet Kazan's many achievements were overshadowed by his betrayal of friends and colleagues in the McCarthy era. Many turned against him. In 1999, when Kazan was to receive a Lifetime Achievement Award at the Academy Awards, Miller was one of the few who stood up for his old friend. "My feelings toward that terrible era are unchanged," Miller said in an article in the *Guardian*, "but at the same time history ought not to be rewritten. Elia Kazan did sufficient extraordinary work in theater and film to merit acknowledgement."[4] Others had not forgotten or forgiven Kazan. During the awards ceremony, hundreds of protestors gathered outside in the streets with signs including this one: "Don't Whitewash the Blacklist."[5]

Red Scare

The McCarthy era was an echo of an earlier anti-Communist hysteria that had similarly wreaked havoc. On November 7, 1919, federal agents launched a series of raids that spread to more than 30 cities across the country. Local police worked with the federal officers to arrest aliens, or noncitizens, and suspected leftists, radicals, anarchists, and Communists. More than 5,000 people were taken into custody; many were held for several months without proper arrest warrants or trials. They were charged with advocating force, violence, and unlawful means to overthrow the government. Most of the people were later released, though in December 1919, nearly 250 of those arrested, including the famous anarchist Emma Goldman, were loaded onto the ship *Buford* and sent to Russia.

The massive arrests became known as the Palmer Raids, after Alexander Mitchell Palmer, the U.S. attorney general under President Woodrow Wilson. Responsible for keeping order and enforcing federal laws, Palmer was responding to the government's fear of insurgency after World War I, which had ended in 1918. Already, Congress had passed a new law, known as the Sedition Act, to silence radicals. The law passed in 1918 made it a crime to speak out against the government, interfere with wartime production, promote the cause of America's enemies, refuse military duty, or advocate any of these activities. Palmer put a young officer in the U.S. Department of Justice named J. Edgar Hoover in charge of rooting out radicals, labor organizers, anarchists who did not believe in government, and Communists. Later, as director of the FBI, Hoover would become one of history's most legendary anti-Communists. Both Hoover and Palmer were reacting to the social pressures of the time, but in retrospect, critics say they were also fanning fears, creating hysteria, and trampling civil rights.

Following the war, the nation faced a crisis of high unemployment, economic uncertainty, and social turmoil. Policemen, miners, and steel workers walked off their jobs in protest of low wages and poor working conditions. Race riots broke out in Omaha and other cities in 1919. An overall feeling of insecurity fueled distrust of any sort of dissent, and the patriotism roused by the war led to xenophobia, or fear of those perceived as outsiders, such as Russian, German, and Italian immigrants. Palmer later explained why he took action. "Like a prairie-fire, the blaze of revolution was sweeping over every American institution of law and order a year ago. It was eating its way into the homes of the American workmen, its sharp tongues of revolutionary heat were licking the altars of the churches . . . burning up the foundations of society."[1] Palmer was especially suspicious of the "Reds," or Communists. Red was the color of the Bolshevik flag, flown by leaders of the recent Communist revolution in Russia, and the years 1919 to 1920 would come to be called the First Red Scare.

After World War I, the U.S. government appointed J. Edgar Hoover to investigate citizens involved in radical or subversive activities. Hoover later became the first director of the Federal Bureau of Investigation (FBI) and one of America's leading opponents of Communism.

THE REDS

Around this time, Communism had begun to take root among a small, but determined, minority of Americans. The word comes from the French word *commun*, meaning "belonging to all." The nineteenth-century German political philosopher Karl Marx is considered the founder of modern Communism, a political and social structure in which there are no social classes and property is commonly shared. In 1848, Marx and the German social scientist and philosopher Friedrich Engels wrote *The Communist Manifesto*, laying out the basic theories of Communism. Communism, as interpreted by Marx and Engels, was also committed to an ongoing revolutionary struggle for change.

Marx's ideas appealed to Vladimir Lenin, a Russian lawyer and radical dissatisfied with the tyranny of the ruling czars in the early twentieth century. He spearheaded a revolution establishing the world's first Communist state. In 1917, the Bolsheviks led by Lenin brought down the government of Czar Nicholas II and began a new Communist-based society that set out to favor workers' rights, land distribution, and peasant rule. Promising peace, land, and bread to the starving, landless Russian people, Lenin in actuality imposed a totalitarian, or dictatorial one-party, government, waging war on dissidents, artists, and intellectuals, as well as on religion, civil rights, and other basic human freedoms.

Lenin's brutal rule over the Russians was not known at first. Inspired by the Bolsheviks, a group of American intellectuals and labor leaders, many of them Russian-born, saw Communism as an improvement over the hardships and inequalities they'd seen with democracy and capitalism. In August 1919, in Chicago, former Socialist Party members founded the American Communist Party and the Communist Labor Party, two organizations that soon merged into the Communist Party (CP) USA, sometimes called the American Communist Party. The CP's core goal was the overthrow of capitalist rule and the capture of power by the working class. As the century unfolded, not all people sympathetic to the Communist movement would join the party, but they would still be considered enemies of the government. Any ties to Communism, even being seen reading its newspaper, the *Daily Worker*, would be considered dangerously un-American.

The American Communists' loyalty to the Soviet Union would prove to be a "fatal flaw,"[2] author Ellen Schrecker notes, as the United States and the Soviet Union became bitter enemies after World War II. The secrecy under which the

CP was forced to operate, because of government disapproval, only contributed to public distrust. To much of mainstream America, particularly leaders in the government, Communists were revolutionaries who wanted to overthrow the government: The Reds should be squashed. Though people might have agreed with this sentiment, not everyone approved of the methods used to curtail the alleged threat. After the raids, a group of 12 prominent lawyers issued a report with stinging indictments, saying that the true danger lay not in a Red revolution but in Palmer's misuse of federal power, including not having arrest or search warrants, lacking proof, and the misuse of force. "Instead of showing me a warrant, they showed me a gun,"[3] one suspect said in the report. As the anti-Communists waged battle in the next decades, the question would become how to balance a citizen's constitutional rights, such as freedom of speech, the right to privacy, and criminal procedures that, for example, shield witnesses from incriminating themselves, with the government's need to protect national security, particularly in times of crisis.

SECOND RED SCARE

The seeds were being planted for the McCarthy era. Patriotic organizations such as the American Legion, a large and passionately anti-Communist organization, started after World War I and would keep fighting Communism into the Cold War. Several Supreme Court decisions on the First Amendment's guarantee of freedom of speech paved the way for a broad use of federal power to suppress unpopular views in later decades, as Ellen Schrecker writes.[4] In the important case *Schenck v. United States* (1919), Supreme Court Justice Oliver Wendell Holmes set out the "clear and present danger" test for free speech. "The question in every case is whether the words used are used in such circumstances and are of such a nature as to create a clear and present danger that they will bring about the substantive evils that Congress has a right to present."[5] For many judges, this measure would rightly or wrongly provide them leeway to suppress the speech of political radicals, including Communists.

This early show of government force against American Communism was a precursor of what was to come in the Second Red Scare in the late 1930s. The general mistrust of Communists had never disappeared, but as the country climbed out of the Great Depression and into World War II, Communists, labor rights activities, and others became targets of suspicion. In 1939, Congress passed the Hatch Act, banning federal employees from joining a political organization that advocated the overthrow of the government. Membership in Communist, as well as many labor, organizations was off-limits to federal workers. The Hatch Act was a response to accusations by Republicans that funds from the federal Works Progress Administration, which put unemployed people to work during the Depression, were used for political lobbying and other purposes by Democrats and labor leaders. The law wound up as another legal weapon that could be used against Communist sympathizers.

In May 1938, Congress created the Special Committee to Investigate Un-American Activities and Propaganda, coined the Dies Committee, after Martin Dies, the conservative Texas Democrat who chaired it from 1938 to 1944. In 1946, the committee would be renamed the House Un-American Activities Committee, or HUAC, and would become a major force for McCarthyism. For seven years, Dies and his committee tirelessly searched out Communists, Nazis, Fascists, and others suspected of so-called un-American activities.

Dies was an opponent of President Franklin D. Roosevelt and the New Deal, a series of government-sponsored job and development programs designed to restore the economy after the Great Depression, because he believed the programs were tainted by Communists. The Dies Committee came to be known for its enthusiastic "red-baiting," or attacking and persecuting people for being Communists. The congressmen investigated hundreds of organizations and government agencies for ties to Communism. Often they used unorthodox tactics. Witnesses were pressured to give names and provide information that implicated others as Communists or Communist sympathizers. If a witness invoked the Fifth Amendment, the constitutional amendment that protects witnesses from being forced to testify against themselves, or even hesitated to answer questions, they were sometimes branded "Red." The committee helped stage raids on local Communist offices, where they took membership lists and tracked down what turned out to be mostly innocent people.

Sometimes they were successful in their attacks. In 1939, the committee investigated Communist Party leader Earl Browder for passport fraud, and he wound up in prison. But the committee often had little evidence to back up its charges. At one point, a committee member accused the popular 11-year-old actress Shirley Temple of Communist sympathies because her signature was on a letter to a French Communist newspaper. Once again, the anti-Communist movement was overreaching, focusing less on actual dangers to national security than on fanning public fears.

The Dies Committee also got involved in labor issues, trying to stop the growth of labor unions. In 1938, the committee charged the Michigan governor with committing treason after he negotiated a labor strike by the United Automobile Workers at the General Motors plant in Flint. Governor Frank Murphy had sent in the National Guard to protect the workers after strikers and police exchanged gunfire, and helped to mediate an agreement that strengthened the bargaining power of the union, defying a court order to punish the strikers. Because this was an election year for Murphy and Congress, Dies sought to structure testimony to suggest that the govenor was responsible for not preventing labor riots. It was also a way to frame Democrats and New Deal supporters in a bad light. This time, President Roosevelt thought that Dies had

Named after the Texas congressman Martin Dies (*seated center, among committee members*), Congress established the Dies Committee to investigate individuals and organizations for Communist activity. In 1946, this committee would be renamed the House Un-American Affairs Committee (HUAC).

gone too far, stating: "I was very much disturbed. I was disturbed not because of the absurdly false charges made by a coterie of disgruntled Republican officeholders against a profoundly religious, able and law abiding Governor; but because a Congressional Committee charged with the responsibility of investigating un-American activities should have permitted itself to be used in a flagrantly unfair and un-American attempt to influence an election."[6]

Yet Roosevelt and other critics of the committee were unable to curtail its crusades and influence. "Dies was unstoppable and HUAC could not be killed,"[7] writes Ellen Schrecker. In 1941, Dies presented a list of 1,121 government workers suspected of belonging to subversive organizations. After an investigation, just three were discharged and one was disciplined. Two years later, he named 39 government employees as subversive; only three lost their jobs, but later the Supreme Court determined even this action was unconstitutional. Despite the poor results of its investigations, the committee, which had been established as temporary, became permanent after Dies left office in January 1945.

THE SMITH ACT AND J. EDGAR HOOVER

After the United States entered World War II in 1941, the country saw an outpouring of patriotism on the home front and increasing suspicion about outsiders, particularly German Americans and Japanese Americans, as well as anyone who criticized the government or the war. In 1940, Congress passed the Smith Act, or Alien Registration Act, which made it a criminal offense for a person to advocate the overthrow of the U.S. government or to be a member of a group that advocated it. The new law was at first directed against antiwar political dissidents, but soon Communists would be targeted, too.

J. Edgar Hoover, who had helped lead the Palmer Raids in 1919, was now director of the FBI, with his eye on destroying the Communist Party. Hoover warned that the Reds had become a major force in all aspects of American life, from radio, movies, and books to churches, schools, colleges, and the government. In 1947, he spoke before the House Un-American Activities Committee and said that "the deceit, trickery, and lies of the American Communists" were as serious as the Soviet threat.[8] In 1948, Hoover suggested that the Smith Act be used to prosecute the Communist Party and to

(continues on page 20)

DENNIS V. UNITED STATES

On July 20, 1948, a labor organizer named Eugene Dennis, who was the general secretary of the American Communist Party, was arrested along with 11 other party leaders. They were charged under the Alien Registration Act, or Smith Act, which made it illegal for anyone to "knowingly or willfully advocate, abet, advise, or teach the duty, necessity, desirability, or propriety of overthrowing or destroying any government in the United States by force or violence, or by the assassination of any officer of any such government."*

As the trial got under way, the charges were hard to prove, since there was no evidence that the defendants had publicly supported violent acts or gathered weapons to start a revolution. The prosecution relied on former members of the Communist Party who testified that the defendants had advocated overthrowing the government. After a trial lasting for 11 months, the defendants were found guilty and sentenced to five years in prison and a $10,000 fine. They appealed the conviction all the way to the U.S. Supreme Court. In the case *Dennis v. United States*, the Supreme Court was asked to decide whether the Smith Act's restrictions on freedom of speech violated the First Amendment.

On June 4, 1951, the Supreme Court ruled 6–2 to uphold the conviction, declaring that it was constitutional to restrict an individual's freedom of speech guaranteed by the First Amendment if the speech posed a threat to the vital security of the country. Chief Justice Fred M. Vinson wrote in the majority decision, "Certainly an attempt to overthrow the Government by force, even though doomed from the outset because of inadequate numbers or power of the revolutionists, is a sufficient evil for Congress to prevent."** The Court held that there is a difference between teaching Communist beliefs and actively advocating those beliefs. The defendants' advocacy of Communist philosophies posed a clear and present danger that

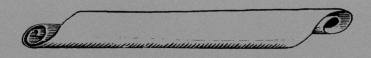

threatened the government and justified the restrictions on the freedom of speech. Because of the seriousness of the consequences,
the probability of success—or whether the defendants would have
been able to overthrow the government—was not a factor in justify-
ing the restrictions on freedom of speech, Vinson wrote.

The decision in *Dennis v. United States* allowed the government
to prosecute Communist Party leaders. "The government had been
waiting impatiently for the decision; now it could go ahead and try
the rest of the party leaders, untold hundreds of them,"*** writes
author Albert Fried. However, a later Supreme Court decision, *Yates
v. United States* in 1957, made parts of the Smith Act unenforceable.
Though the law remains today, the Smith Act has not been used to
prosecute people. Even in 1951, two justices strongly disagreed with
the majority opinion. In his eloquent dissent, Justice Hugo Black,
supported by Justice William O. Douglass, vehemently defended the
rights of the defendants to assemble, talk, and publish their ideas:

> At the outset, I want to emphasize what the crime involved
> in this case is, and what it is not. These petitioners were not
> charged with an attempt to overthrow the Government. They
> were not charged with overt acts of any kind designed to
> overthrow the Government. They were not even charged with
> saying anything or writing anything designed to overthrow the
> Government. The charge was that they agreed to assemble
> and to talk and publish certain ideas at a later date: the
> indictment is that they conspired to organize the Communist
> Party and to use speech or newspapers and other publica-
> tions in the future to teach and advocate the forcible over-
> throw of the Government. No matter how it is worded, this

(continues)

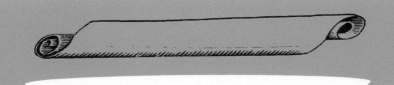

(continued)

is a virulent form of prior censorship of speech and press, which I believe the First Amendment forbids . . .

. . . Undoubtedly a governmental policy of unfettered communication of ideas does entail dangers. To the Founders of this Nation, however, the benefits derived from free expression were worth the risk. They embodied this philosophy in the First Amendment's command that "Congress shall make no law . . . abridging the freedom of speech, or of the press. . . ." I have always believed that the First Amendment is the keystone of our Government, that the freedoms it guarantees provide the best insurance against destruction of all freedom . . .

. . . Public opinion being what it now is, few will protest the conviction of these Communist petitioners. There is hope, however, that, in calmer times, when present pressures, passions and fears subside, this or some later Court will restore the First Amendment liberties to the high preferred place where they belong in a free society.****

---

* *Dennis v. United States*, Cornell University Law School, Legal Information Institute. Supreme Court Collection. URL: http://supct.law.cornell.edu/supct/html/historics/USSC_CR_0341_0494_ZO.html.
** Ibid.
*** Albert Fried, *McCarthyism: The Great American Red Scare: A Documentary History*. New York: Oxford University Press, 1997, p. 110.
**** *Dennis v. United States*, Cornell University Law School.

(continued from page 17)

put party leaders in jail. The FBI put together a massive legal brief to establish that the Communist Party was illegal and began to round up party leaders. On July 20, 1948, a grand jury in New York indicted 12 party leaders, including Eugene Dennis, though one took ill. The trial of the 11, which started in the fall and lasted into the following spring, made national headlines. Noisy picketers surrounded the courthouse. Chaos seemed ready to erupt.

LOYALTY IN THE COLD WAR

Many American Communists and sympathizers left the Communist Party in 1938 after the Soviet Union signed a nonaggression pact with Nazi Germany. They were outraged by the Soviets' willingness to negotiate with Fascist Germany under its leader, Adolf Hitler. Soon, however, the tables turned again. During World War II, after Germany invaded Russia in 1941, the Soviets joined the United States and its allies, forging a temporary friendship between the two nations, and the American Communist Party's membership roster grew for several years. This heyday for the party lasted only through the war, which concluded with an Allied victory in 1945. With the war's end, the fragile alliance between the Soviets and Americans was over.

After World War II, Western countries watched nervously as the Soviet Communist government expanded its sphere of influence into Eastern Europe, taking control of Poland, Czechoslovakia, and Hungary. Communism was spreading fast, and the world was quickly dividing into Communist and non-Communist. A new war was beginning. This one was not waged on the battlefield or fought with tanks and guns. The Cold War was a conflict of ideology—democracy versus Communism—and it put the world on edge.

In the next years, the Cold War would dominate not only world politics but also the internal politics of the United States. It would last from the end of World War II until 1989 with the collapse of the Berlin Wall. In the late 1940s, however, the dawning of the Cold War meant that American Communists were more feared than ever before—even though, at the same time, the American Communist Party was weaker. After President

Roosevelt died in office on April 12, 1945, he was replaced by Democrat Harry S. Truman, his vice president. President Truman was not as liberal as Roosevelt and was no friend to organized labor or to Communists. Determined to prove that he was as much of an anti-Communist as the more conservative Republicans who had swept the House and Senate in the 1946 elections, Truman moved quickly to show his toughness against the Soviets and Communism within the United States.

In March 1947, President Truman signed Executive Order 9835, known as the Loyalty Order, creating a loyalty review program for federal employees. Across the country, loyalty review boards looked into the private lives of government workers, checking out their political beliefs, friends, acquaintances, and memberships in organizations, and making sure they had no ties at all to Communism. To avoid trouble, organizations and corporations began to get rid of people they suspected had Communist sympathies. More than 3 million employees of the federal government were investigated for Communist connections. Of those, only a few hundred were fired, indicating that most were guilty of nothing at all. Still, thousands more resigned, outraged by the investigations' probe of their personal lives and worried about their loss of privacy.

The
Hollywood Ten

The movie *Woman of the Year,* starring Spencer Tracy and Katharine Hepburn, was a popular hit when it came out in 1942. The story is about two rival reporters who fall in love and get married, only to fight jealously. The screenwriter Ring Lardner Jr., who wrote the fast-paced, funny script, won an Oscar for the film, which would become a Hollywood classic and is still shown regularly on television. Five years later, however, Lardner, one of Hollywood's highest-paid screenwriters, was on his way to jail, captured in the anti-Communism net sweeping through the film industry. He had refused to testify before the House Un-American Activities Committee (HUAC) in its 1947 investigation into Communism in the film industry. Lardner was subsequently blacklisted and unable to work in Hollywood for nearly two decades.

Communism did have followers in Hollywood. Lardner was one of many in the film industry who had at one time or another believed in left-wing causes or supported anti-Fascist organizations. Some writers, actors, directors, and others in Hollywood were attracted to Communism because of its opposition to the Fascism in Nazi Germany, as well as its commitment to social justice, labor unions, workers' rights, and other issues close to their hearts. Writers who were Communists or supported Communism helped form the Screen Writers Guild, the union representing the writers' of Hollywood films, and established writers' groups, magazines, and theater companies, as Ellen Schrecker writes in *Many Are the Crimes*.[1] Before World War II, being part of a Communist organization could sometimes help a young writer's career by providing contacts and support in breaking into the business. Sometimes writers, actors, and others in the film industry infused their work with their political beliefs. John Howard Lawson, a playwright, was a leader of the Hollywood Communists and urged actors to try to advance the class struggle in their work. "If you are an extra in a street scene of a tenement district or any poor surroundings, play your part to excite sympathy,"[2] he said. Wealthy Hollywood writers and actors also contributed money to the Communist Party and supported the party's causes, such as improving labor conditions for farm workers.

In 1947, the congressmen who sat on HUAC decided to investigate whether Communists were infiltrating the film industry and spreading Communist propaganda. The FBI did its part, as well, providing a report on Communism in Hollywood, with a list of people who were allegedly present or former members of the Communist Party and a list of friendly witnesses. The chair of HUAC was Republican congressman J. Parnell Thomas, a conservative from New Jersey who was a staunch anti-Communist. Thomas had made a trip to California to investigate whether Communists were involved in the Screen Writers Guild and trying to slip Communist ideas into their scripts. He was determined to put a stop to this.

HEARINGS

The House committee sent subpoenas to 43 people, mostly friendly witnesses such as the actor Ronald Reagan, who was the president of the Screen Actors Guild, and the popular actor Gary Cooper, who supported the committee's efforts. When they appeared before HUAC in Washington, D.C., many of the friendly witnesses divulged information on people they thought were Communists or Communist sympathizers. In his testimony to HUAC, Reagan said, "There has been a small group within the Screen Actors Guild which has consistently opposed the policy of the guild board and officers of the guild, as evidenced by the vote on various issues. That small clique referred to has been suspected of more or less following the tactics that we associate with the Communist Party."[3]

Nineteen subpoenas were for unfriendly witnesses, including party members, but also others who were not Communists. The witnesses hired a team of lawyers and debated about whether to cooperate with the committee. They did not really know what would happen if they refused to answer questions such as this one: "Are you now or have you ever been a member of the Communist Party?"[4] Meanwhile, a group of Hollywood stars led by actors Lauren Bacall and Humphrey Bogart organized the Committee for the First Amendment to support their colleagues. Members included Lucille Ball, Frank Sinatra, Gene Kelly, Burt Lancaster, and others. The group was not supporting Communism but rather defending the film industry.

Once the hearings began, the witnesses had to decide what questions to answer or not. Some testified against Communists, naming names of people they thought were Communists or Communist sympathizers. Ten witnesses refused to testify. They were Alvah Bessie, Herbert Biberman, Lester Cole, Edward

In 1947, HUAC began investigating people for using the film industry to promote Communism in America. The Hollywood Ten (*above, with their attorneys*) refused to give testimony to HUAC. Ring Lardner Jr. stands in the top row, far left.

Dmytryk, Ring Lardner Jr., John Howard Lawson, Albert Maltz, Samuel Ornitz, Adrian Scott, and Dalton Trumbo. Claiming that the First Amendment gave them the right to refuse to testify, the 10 would not budge. In the end, they were found guilty of contempt of Congress.

Fearing that the film industry would be tarnished and suffer financial damage, Hollywood's leaders refused to stand behind the 10 defendants. The Screen Actors Guild, the union representing actors, voted to make its officers swear they were not Communists. "If any actor by his own actions . . . has so offended American public opinion that he has made himself unsalable at the box office, the Guild cannot and would not want to force any employer to hire him."[5] After the House of Representatives voted to support HUAC's actions against the Hollywood Ten, film industry executives met at the Waldorf-Astoria Hotel in New York to decide how to respond. They issued the Waldorf Statement on December 3, 1947, declaring that the 10 would be fired or suspended without pay until they were cleared of charges and swore they were not Communists. In effect, they were blacklisted, deemed subversive and banned from working. The statement read in part:

> Members of the Association of Motion Picture Producers deplore the action of the ten Hollywood men who have been cited for contempt. We do not desire to prejudge their legal rights, but their actions have been a disservice to their employers and have impaired their usefulness to the industry . . . we will not re-employ any of the ten until such time as he has acquitted or purged himself of contempt and declares under oath that he is not a Communist.[6]

The 10 exhausted their appeals and were sent to prison to serve one-year sentences. One of them, film director Edward Dmytryk, decided to admit that he was briefly a member of the Communist Party and agreed to name names. He was released from jail early and identified 26 people he said were involved in radical groups. He also said he was forced to put Communist propaganda in his films. Because of his confession, he was soon able to work again. When the other nine had served their sentences, they were blacklisted and not able to find work.

The blacklist did not stop with them. All 19 of the unfriendly witnesses were blacklisted. Even witnesses who had

(continues on page 30)

THE TESTIMONY OF WALT DISNEY

Born in Chicago in 1901 and raised on a farm in Missouri, Walt Disney came to Hollywood with $40 in his pocket, a talent for sketching cartoons, and an animated film that he had made. He started a movie production business with his brother. His soon-to-be-famous character Mickey Mouse appeared in Disney's first hit, *Steamboat Willie*, an animated movie, in 1928.

Disney was soon turning out celebrated full-length animated films, including *Snow White and the Seven Dwarfs* in 1937, followed by *Pinocchio*, *Fantasia*, and *Bambi*. His studio in Burbank, California, employed more than a thousand people and would eventually win 48 Academy Awards. He also staked out his views on labor and politics. In the early 1940s, Disney refused to bargain with the Cartoonists' Guild, the union representing cartoonists, which went on strike. A conservative who was against organized labor, Disney claimed that Communist agitation had brought about the strike and that there was a Communist conspiracy in Hollywood.

During World War II, Disney's studio produced patriotic films to support the war effort. Disney and a few others formed the Motion Picture Alliance for the Preservation of American Ideals in 1944. The organization was made up of conservative movie industry workers who wanted to stop what they perceived as the infiltration of Communists into Hollywood. One member was future president Ronald Reagan.

In 1947, Disney testified as a friendly witness before HUAC about Communists in Hollywood. The following are two excerpts from the hearing, where Disney was being interrogated by HUAC investigator H.A. Smith.

Smith: Do you have any people in your studio at the present time that you believe are Communist or Fascist, employed there?

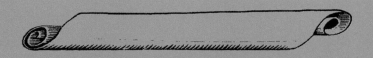

Disney: No; at the present time I feel that everybody in my studio is one-hundred-percent American.

Smith: Have you had at any time, in your opinion, in the past, have you at any time in the past had any Communists employed at your studio?

Disney: Yes; in the past I had some people that I definitely feel were Communists.

Smith: As a matter of fact, Mr. Disney, you experienced a strike at your studio, did you not?

Disney: Yes.

Smith: And is it your opinion that that strike was instituted by members of the Communist Party to serve their purposes?

Disney: Well, it proved itself so with time, and I definitely feel it was a Communist group trying to take over my artists and they did take them over.

Chairman J. Parnell Thomas: Do you say they did take them over?

Disney: They did take them over.

(And later . . .)

Smith: Can you name any other individuals that were active at the time of the strike that you believe in your opinion are Communists?

Disney: Well, I feel that there is one artist in my plant, that came in there, he came in about 1938, and he sort of stayed in the background, he wasn't too active, but he was the real brains of this, and I believe he is a Communist. His name is David Hilberman.

Smith: How is it spelled?

Disney: H-i-l-b-e-r-m-a-n, I believe. I looked into his record and I found that, number 1, that he had no religion and, number 2,

(continues)

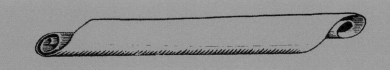

(continued)

that he had spent considerable time at the Moscow Art Theatre studying art direction, or something.

Smith: Any others, Mr. Disney?

Disney: Well, I think Sorrell is sure tied up with them. If he isn't a Communist, he sure should be one.

Smith: Do you remember the name of William Pomerance, did he have anything to do with it?

Disney: Yes, sir. He came in later. Sorrell put him in charge as business manager of cartoonists and later he went to the Screen Actors as their business agent, and in turn he put in another man by the name of Maurice Howard, the present business agent. And they are all tied up with the same outfit.

Smith: What is your opinion of Mr. Pomerance and Mr. Howard as to whether or not they are or are not Communists?

Disney: In my opinion they are Communists. No one has any way of proving those things.

Smith: Were you able to produce during the strike?

Disney: Yes, I did, because there was a very few, very small majority that was on the outside, and all the other unions ignored all the lines because of the setup of the thing.

Smith: What is your personal opinion of the Communist Party, Mr. Disney, as to whether or not it is a political party?

(continued from page 27)

testified reluctantly against their colleagues were blacklisted, like Larry Parks, an actor who finally broke down in front of HUAC and gave names. Others in Hollywood who were known

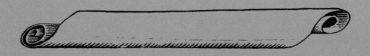

Disney: Well, I don't believe it is a political party. I believe it is an un-American thing. The thing that I resent the most is that they are able to get into these unions, take them over, and represent to the world that a group of people that are in my plant, that I know are good, one-hundred-percent Americans, are trapped by this group, and they are represented to the world as supporting all of those ideologies, and it is not so, and I feel that they really ought to be smoked out and shown up for what they are, so that all of the good, free causes in this country, all the liberalisms that really are American, can go out without the taint of communism. That is my sincere feeling on it.

Smith: Do you feel that there is a threat of Communism in the motion-picture industry?

Disney: Yes, there is, and there are many reasons why they would like to take it over or get in and control it, or disrupt it, but I don't think they have gotten very far, and I think the industry is made up of good Americans, just like in my plant, good, solid Americans. My boys have been fighting it longer than I have. They are trying to get out from under it and they will in time if we can just show them up.[*]

---

[*] Laura M. Miller, "The Testimony of Walter E. Disney Before the House Committee on Un-American Activities (24 October 1947)," *Dictionary of American History.* The Gale Group Inc., 2003. Encyclopedia.com. http://www.encyclopedia.com/doc/1G2-3401804827.html.

to be friends of them, or were leftists, or had even distant ties to the Communist Party also lost their jobs. The blacklist eventually included more than 400 people, including workers in movies, television, and radio. Some of them used pseudonyms to continue working in their fields. "Others have had to find new occupations entirely, among them carpentry, selling women's clothing, bartending, driving a school bus, and waiting on tables in a restaurant,"[7] wrote Lardner in 1961.

After Lardner was released from jail, he could not work in the film industry, so he wrote a novel instead. He moved to England, worked under a pseudonym on television series, and wrote for movies where he received no credits. Finally in 1965, Lardner's name appeared in the screen credits of *The Cincinnati Kid*. He won his second Academy Award for writing the screenplay for the classic movie *M*A*S*H* in 1970. Still, like the many others who had been blacklisted, Lardner would never get back the many years of his working life that had been lost.

A SPY IN THE STATE DEPARTMENT

The hunt for Communists had heated up. At the helm of the FBI, J. Edgar Hoover amassed thousands of surveillance reports on people, a list that would grow to include First Lady Eleanor Roosevelt, scientist Albert Einstein, and later Marilyn Monroe and even President John F. Kennedy. By 1960, the FBI had 432,000 open files on subversives, according to Hoover biographer Kenneth D. Ackerman. Hoover kept his records highly secret, some of them even labeled personal and confidential, in order that he had total control over them. When it was time, he launched investigations.

One of his targets was Alger Hiss, a former high-ranking State Department lawyer who was rumored to be a Soviet agent. In the early 1940s, the FBI had begun surveillance, using wiretaps and other electronic devices, to monitor Hiss and his wife, Priscilla, but did not find evidence of spying. Nevertheless, the pressure on Hiss led him to resign from his job as an official at the United Nations, an organization that he had helped start, and take a job in the private sector as president of the Carnegie Endowment for International Peace.

Then in 1948, a former colleague at the State Department testified against him before HUAC.

The charges were leveled by Whittaker Chambers, a *Time*
magazine editor who admitted to being a past member of the
Communist Party. Chambers accused Hiss of being a Soviet
spy who supplied Soviet agents with classified U.S. documents
during the 1930s. Chambers testified before HUAC on August
3, 1948, that Hiss was a Communist and involved in espionage
while employed by the federal government. Chambers had
already admitted that he participated in espionage and was
a cooperating witness against Hiss. The State Department
leaped to Hiss's defense. But in the end, Chambers provided
evidence that he had hidden in a pumpkin on his farm in
Maryland. The evidence included five rolls of microfilm
containing government documents, handwritten notes from
Hiss, and State Department papers that seemed to confirm
Chambers's accusations.

Hiss was brought before HUAC in August 1948 to
respond, and he denied the charges, but one congressman in
particular was not convinced. The California congressman
Richard M. Nixon had used his anti-Communist views to help
win his first election in 1946, and anti-Communism would
be a refrain during his long political career. Nixon questioned
Chambers in secret again. Then Hiss had to appear before
HUAC a second time in September. Nixon's interrogation of
Hiss kept the case alive and convinced others on the committee that they could not let it go, despite the lack of hard
evidence. Hiss was indicted by a federal grand jury, not for
espionage—the statute of limitations had run out for those
charges—but for perjury, or lying to HUAC. After one mis-
trial, Hiss was tried again and found guilty in January 1950 of
two counts of perjury. He served 44 months of two five-year
sentences in a federal prison.

Hiss's trial fueled contentious debate, not just over the exis-
tence of Communists and espionage in the federal government

When cartoonists at his movie studio went on strike, celebrated animator Walt Disney publicly blamed the growing influence of Communism in Hollywood. Disney, an antilabor conservative, would later name suspected Communists in Hollywood during his HUAC testimony (*above*).

but also over the fairness and legality of such a trial during the height of the Cold War. Controversy over Hiss's guilt or innocence would continue for decades. Hiss insisted that he was innocent all the way until his death in 1996. It was only after the Soviets in the 1990s released archives from the Cold War that more information became known about Hiss. The archives contained documents that described a Soviet agent with the code name of "AMES" who was likely Alger Hiss. Most historians now believe that Hiss was probably a Soviet spy. In the short term, however, the Hiss verdict fueled both hysteria about Soviet spies in the government and anger from those who believed that Hiss was an innocent victim of the anti-Communist paranoia sweeping the country. The country was bitterly dividing.

ALDER V. BOARD OF EDUCATION

It wasn't just Hollywood stars and State Department officials who were arrested, blacklisted, or simply not hired during the Second Red Scare. The government also investigated Communist infiltration in the education system. College professors and public school teachers were brought before the Senate Internal Security Subcommittee and grilled about their backgrounds and affiliations. Many states took steps to remove alleged Communists from the classrooms. In California, state university professors were forced to take loyalty oaths, pledging that they were not members of the Communist Party; if they refused, they were fired.

In 1949, New York passed the Feinberg Law, allowing schools to dismiss teachers who belonged to organizations that were deemed subversive. The New York City schools superintendent called in teachers, asking them whether they were or had ever been members of the Communist Party. Many of the accused teachers wound up in front of a Senate subcommittee established to monitor and enforce the 1950 McCarran Internal Security Act that clamped down on Communists. The teachers often refused to answer questions. One teacher was so distraught at being called out of her classroom and asked if she was a Communist that she committed suicide. Not all teachers refused to cooperate. A teacher and union official named Dr. Bella Dodd, a former Communist Party member, gave a list with the names of 100 teachers she claimed were party members.

One of the 378 New York City teachers who lost their jobs under the Feinberg Law was Irving Adler, the son of Polish immigrants. In fact, Adler, the mathematics director in the city schools, was a member of the Communist Party. He later left the CP after he learned about the human rights abuses in the Soviet Union, but he remained sympathetic to Communism. Like other teachers, Adler refused to answer questions, maintaining that he was protected by the civil service laws that prohibited employees from being asked about their political affiliations. Nonetheless, he was fired for insubordination and conduct unbecoming a teacher.

The New York Teachers Union challenged the constitutionality of the Feinberg Law. The teachers won initially, but the case was appealed and, in 1952, the U.S. Supreme Court decided 6–3 against the teachers in *Alder v. Board of Education*. For the majority decision, Justice Sherman Minton stated,

> A teacher works in a sensitive area in a school room. There he shapes the attitude of young minds towards the society in which they live. In this, the state has a vital concern. It must preserve the integrity of the schools. That the school authorities have the right and the duty to screen the officials, teachers, and employees as to their fitness to maintain the integrity of the schools as a part of ordered society, cannot be doubted. One's associates, past and present, as well as one's conduct, may properly be considered in determining fitness and loyalty. From time immemorial, one's reputation has been determined in part by the company he keeps. In the employment of officials and teachers of the school system, the state may very properly inquire into the company they keep, and we know of no rule, constitutional or otherwise, that prevents the state, when determining the fitness and loyalty of such persons, from considering the organizations and persons with whom they associate.[8]

Three justices disagreed, including William O. Douglas. In his dissent, he wrote: "The present law proceeds on a principle repugnant to our society—guilt by association . . . What happens under this law is typical of what happens in a police state. Teachers are under constant surveillance; their pasts are combed for signs of disloyalty; their utterances are watched for clues to dangerous thoughts."[9] In 1967, the Supreme Court in a new case reversed the decision. Adler and the other teachers who had been fired sued to get their jobs back. Adler, who had moved to Vermont and become a prolific author of books for children and adults, got his pension reinstated.

Elmer Davis, a popular radio commentator, did not fear speaking out against the Red Scare. He said that movements to rout out teachers were a "general attack not only on schools and colleges and libraries, on teachers and textbooks, but on all people who think and write . . . in short, on the freedom of the mind."[10] Some of the charges during these investigations were, in fact, true—or partially true. Yet even if some of the people accused were indeed members of the Communist Party, did they pose a real threat to society? Or were they persecuted simply for unpopular beliefs, friendships, or interests? Those questions would be debated for decades to come, but back in the early 1950s, more trouble lay ahead.

The Senator
from Wisconsin

On February 9, 1950, a heavyset senator from Wisconsin stood behind the podium at the Lincoln Day dinner in Wheeling, West Virginia. Senator Joseph R. McCarthy, a tall man with bushy eyebrows, looked out at a crowd of loyal Republican Party members. In a dramatic gesture, McCarthy held up a piece of paper and spoke. "I have in my hand a list of 205—a list of names that were made known to the Secretary of State as being members of the Communist Party and who, nevertheless, are still working and shaping policy in the State Department,"[1] McCarthy declared. With those words, he shook the nation—even though it was soon apparent that his facts were inaccurate, bordering on lies.

Though reporters were present, the exact words of McCarthy's speech are not known today; a tape that recorded them was erased. The number of names actually on McCarthy's

Senator Joseph R. McCarthy, a relatively unknown Republican from Wisconsin, received national attention when he accused the government of employing Communists. McCarthy used fear to publicly ruin the lives of many American citizens in his anti-Communist crusade.

list remains uncertain—or whether he even had a list. The next day he told reporters in Salt Lake City that there were 57 Communists, and he told the Senate more than a week later that there were 81. He backed away from whether they were really Communists, saying that maybe they had Communist connections. Nonetheless, the impact of McCarthy's charges fed on the Cold War climate of panic and fear. It almost didn't matter whether McCarthy had based his allegations on known facts or on undocumented hearsay, or if he had even made them up entirely. He succeeded in setting off a firestorm of alarm.

The Associated Press picked up the story, and 30 newspapers published it. From Wheeling, McCarthy continued on his five-city tour. At each stop, reporters interviewed him and newspapers published his charges, spreading his accusations like wildfire, despite the changing facts. McCarthy even sent a telegram to the White House warning that information on disloyal people in the State Department must be released. "Failure on your part will label the Democratic party of being the bedfellow of international Communism," he wrote.[2] Outraged, the State Department repeatedly denied his charges, and President Harry Truman responded with a telegram that may or may not have been sent but that has been preserved: "Your telegram is not only not true . . . It shows conclusively that you are not even fit to have a hand in the operation of the Government of the United States."[3]

McCarthy may not have earned much recognition during his first Senate term, but he was suddenly catapulted into the national spotlight and on his way to becoming one of the most well-known faces in the country. McCarthy's anti-Communist crusade, which was only just getting started, would take a tremendous toll in the next few years, driving wedges between Democrats and Republicans, paralyzing the government, and tearing apart the country. Yet even at the beginning, it was apparent to many that McCarthy did not always have the facts to back up his charges.

FROM CHICKEN FARMER TO U.S. SENATOR

For a man who was to become famous for his extremism, brazen bullying, and love of the limelight, McCarthy rose up from very modest Midwestern roots. Joseph Raymond McCarthy was born on November 14, 1908, and grew up on his family's 142-acre (57.4 hectare) farm near Grand Chute, Wisconsin. He was the fifth of nine children of Timothy and Bridget (Tierney) McCarthy, who were devout Catholics. Timothy was half Irish and half German, and Bridget had emigrated from Ireland with her family.

The large family struggled to make a meager living from the land. McCarthy attended a one-room school through the eighth grade. Some biographers say that McCarthy was a shy boy who was teased a lot, causing his mother to be over-protective of her favorite son, but little is actually known of his childhood experiences. When he was 14, McCarthy left school. Using money he had saved up, he bought 50 chickens and rented a little land from his father. Soon he was running a prosperous chicken farm with thousands of chickens. But after McCarthy fell ill with pneumonia, the chicken business failed. He moved to a nearby town and took a job as manager of a supermarket.

Though his parents weren't formally educated, McCarthy decided to go back to school. He entered high school at the age of 19 and studied so hard that he was able to graduate in one year. He went on to Marquette University, a Jesuit school in Milwaukee. He was on the college boxing team and turned out to be a good boxer. He would later look at himself as a prize-fighter, doing humble battle for the folks in America. His supporters would think of him as a fearless slugger, always willing to lay the first and the last punch.

McCarthy graduated in 1935 and became a lawyer. In 1939, he was elected a circuit judge. At age 33, McCarthy joined the U.S. Marine Corps and fought without distinction in World War II. When he came home from the war, he decided to enter politics and run for the U.S. Senate as a Republican.

In the Republican primary, McCarthy faced Robert M. La Follette Jr., a member of a prominent Wisconsin political family and a former three-term senator for a third party. La Follette had rejoined the Republican Party, and now the voters had to choose between a popular politician and McCarthy, a circuit court judge with a lackluster war record. Facing down the odds, and backed by the Wisconsin Republican Party, McCarthy won the primary and went on to beat the Democratic candidate in a landslide.

McCarthy was only 38 years old when he arrived in Washington, D.C., in 1947. He was the youngest U.S. senator and a bachelor, and he found it difficult to get a foothold or gain recognition. As a first-term senator, McCarthy had little clout and did not make much of a stir. That November, President Truman, a Democrat, won reelection to a second term, and the Democrats also won a majority in the Senate, putting McCarthy and the Republicans in the minority. Already, McCarthy was rubbing some people the wrong way, ignoring Senate rules and traditions, and coming on too aggressively. The chairman of the Banking and Currency Committee refused to take his chair if McCarthy sat on his committee, so the Republicans on the committee pushed him out.

A CLIMATE OF FEAR

By February 1950, McCarthy was nearing the end of his first term in the Senate. He hadn't made his mark in Washington, and he needed an issue that would excite Republicans and win him votes in his reelection. By taking on Communism, McCarthy found an issue that he must have thought would bring him power and prestige, as well as enemies and controversy. He seemed to be looking for all of the above. On February 20, 1950, just weeks after his speech in Wheeling, McCarthy stood on the Senate floor and gave a lengthy speech, repeating his charges of Communists in the State Department, even though the numbers kept changing.

The Senate formed a subcommittee to investigate whether McCarthy's accusations had merit. Led by Senator Millard Tydings, a veteran Democrat from Maryland, the committee was charged with investigating disloyalty among State Department employees. The Tydings Committee met from March 8 to June 28, 1950. McCarthy did not have all the names of those in his original charges, so he gave the committee a handful of new names, mostly people already investigated but not found to be Communists. One of the accused by McCarthy was Owen Lattimore, a professor at the Johns Hopkins University, who was an advisor on U.S. policy toward China. McCarthy accused Lattimore of being a Communist and a "top Russian spy,"[4] but an FBI report could not find any evidence of this at the time. In 1952, Lattimore was indicted for perjury on charges that he had lied when he said that he had not promoted Communism; those charges were later dismissed, as well.

The Tydings Committee was split between Republicans and Democrats, and it became a partisan fight. In the end, Tydings issued a report finding no evidence of Communism in the State Department and indicted McCarthy, calling his charges "a fraud and a hoax."[5] McCarthy bit back, saying the report was giving a green light to Communism. Other Republicans backed McCarthy. Republican senator William Jenner said Tydings was guilty of "the most scandalous and brazen whitewash of treasonable conspiracy in our history."[6] Soon after, McCarthy turned his focus on Tydings himself and campaigned so hard against him that Tydings lost his next election. McCarthy also continued to accuse the State Department of employing disloyal workers.

A group of more moderate Republicans decided that they couldn't sit still and watch. In June, Senator Margaret Chase Smith of Maine said in a "Declaration of Conscience" on the Senate floor that McCarthy's tactics had lowered the Senate to a forum for character assassination and hate. "Those of us who shout the loudest about Americanism . . . are all too frequently those who, by our own words and acts, ignore some of the basic principles of Americanism: The right to criticize; The right to hold unpopular beliefs; The right to protest; The right of independent thought."[7] Smith added she wanted "the nation to recapture the strength and unity it once had when we fought the enemy instead of ourselves."[8] Six other Republicans gave their support to this attack on McCarthy, but they were a small

(continues on page 46)

The political cartoonist Herbert Block, known as Herblock, used his art and commentary to fight the climate of fear and suspicion during the anti-Communist crusades. In his cartoons appearing in the *Washington Post*, Herblock was a relentless critic of the HUAC, which he saw as a threat on civil liberties. On March 29, 1950, he published a landmark cartoon in the *Washington Post* that showed men holding onto an elephant, a symbol of the Republican Party, being dragged helplessly toward a stack of buckets filled with tar, topped with a barrel called "McCarthyism." The elephant says, "You mean I'm supposed to stand on that?"* With his cartoon, Herblock introduced the term "McCarthyism" into the public domain, a word that came to mean the use of unfair allegations and personal attacks to defame a person's character and reputation because of political differences. McCarthy would take hold of the label, too, and wear it with some pride.

Herblock was born in Chicago in 1909. He quit college to join the *Chicago News* as an editorial cartoonist in 1929. One of his favorite topics was the protection of civil liberties. Block was appalled to see lives ruined and reputations smeared by anti-Communist crusades that sometimes went too far. In December 1938, Herblock drew a Christmas cartoon warning against unconstitutional attacks on civil liberties by the House Special Committee to Investigate Un-American Activities and Propaganda. Using satire, Herblock suggested the committee saw even Santa Claus as a subversive threat.

In 1947, he wrote a cartoon, titled "It's okay—We're hunting Communists," showing a car, with "Committee on Un-American Activities" written on its trunk, plowing down people on a crowded street. In a cartoon titled "Fire!" published in the *Washington Post* on June 17, 1949, Herblock showed a man labeled "Hysteria" carrying

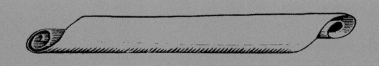

a bucket of water up a ladder to put out the flame of the Statue of Liberty. The message was that, in their effort to stamp out subversion, the anti-Communists were also threatening American liberties. When anti-Communist campaigns went after public school teachers and many lost their jobs, he published a cartoon with the words, "You read books, eh?" showing a teacher at her desk, surrounded by men destroying her classroom.**

While many others who hated McCarthy were too cautious to take a stand, Herblock continued to fearlessly publish cartoons. In 1952, Herblock criticized McCarthy's attacks on the Truman administration during the Korean War. When the State Department asked Herblock to distribute a booklet of anti-Communist cartoons abroad to support the war effort, McCarthy tried to attack the cartoonist by accusing him of being paid by the administration. Herblock just kept writing and drawing. After Dwight D. Eisenhower took office in 1953, Herblock attacked the new president's unwillingness to take on McCarthy. In 1954, he published a cartoon about an accusation by the anti-Communist American Legion that the Girl Scouts were un-American. Using his trademark combination of humor and bite, Herblock wrote, "Stand fast, men—They're armed with marshmallows."***

After his death in 2001, Herblock's personal archives were donated to the Library of Congress, which has posted an exhibit online showing his unforgettable cartoons. The exhibit can be viewed at http://www.loc.gov/rr/print/swann/herblock/fire.html.

---

* "Herblock's History: Political Cartoons from the Crash to the Millennium," Library of Congress Exhibition. http://www.loc.gov/rr/print/swann/herblock/fire.html.
** Ibid.
*** Ibid.

(continued from page 43)
minority. Most Republicans were lining up behind him, just as Democrats were also afraid to take a stand against him.

KOREAN WAR

As McCarthy continued his ascent into the public consciousness, the Cold War was at its height and the fear of Communism, both inside the United States and abroad, was on the rise. Just a month before McCarthy's speech in February 1950, Alger Hiss was convicted of perjury in connection with accusations of being a Soviet spy. Internationally, Communism appeared to be spreading. In the fall of 1949, the long and brutal civil war in China had ended with a Communist victory. On October 1, 1949, Chinese Communist leader Mao Tse-tung proclaimed the establishment of the People's Republic of China, forcing Chiang Kai-shek and his Nationalist Chinese followers to retreat from mainland China to the island of Taiwan.

The Soviet Union, the strongest Communist power at that time, was also flexing its muscles. On August 29, 1949, the Soviets exploded their first atomic bomb, which came as a terrible shock to the American public. The Soviets' nuclear capabilities were until that time unknown, and the explosion increased anxiety about the Communist threat. In addition to all this, tension was rising on the Korean peninsula between the Communists in the North and non-Communists in the South. The tension would soon erupt into the Korean War and bring American soldiers into a direct confrontation against Communism, giving McCarthy another piece of ammunition in his Red Scare.

On June 25, 1950, North Korean troops invaded South Korea, setting off an international crisis over the spread of Communism. After World War II, the Korean peninsula had been divided along the 38th parallel into Soviet and U.S. occupation zones. Separate governments were established: the democratic Republic of Korea in the south and the Communist

People's Democratic Republic of Korea in the north. Now as the North Korean People's Army, armed with Russian tanks and weapons, moved swiftly southward, the United Nations condemned the Communist forces, branding them as the aggressors, and called for aid to South Korea. On June 27, President Truman authorized American air, naval, and ground troops to assist South Korea. Fifteen other United Nations (UN) member nations also sent troops. Together, the international troops were led by supreme commander General Douglas MacArthur—a man McCarthy would later accuse, falsely, of treason.

Some 1.8 million American soldiers fought in Korea, and more than 36,000 were killed before an armistice agreement was signed on July 27, 1953. While the war raged overseas, the fear of the Communist menace at home grew stronger. Congressional Democrats and Republicans teamed up to pass the McCarran Internal Security Act, a federal anti-Communism law named after Senator Patrick A. McCarran, a Democrat from Nevada. The law required that Communist organizations register with the Department of Justice. It strengthened the ability of the United States to both exclude and deport Communists and other subversives. Also, people trained in espionage had to register with the government. Critics of the law, including President Truman, claimed that it interfered with civil liberties and would only help the Communists because it mocked the Bill of Rights. He vetoed the bill, but Congress overrode his veto and the McCarran Internal Security Act was enacted in September 1950. The law was later challenged in the courts and declared unconstitutional.

TAKING DOWN A JOURNALIST

One of the few people who spoke up against McCarthy that year was Drew Pearson, a *Baltimore Sun* columnist and radio broadcaster who devoted much of his commentary to attacking McCarthy. After McCarthy made his speech in Wheeling, Pearson wrote that "every man on the McCarthy list has already

The Cold War helped incite fears of Communists and espionage in the American public. Alger Hiss (*above center*) was a government official who had helped establish the United Nations when he was accused of being a Soviet spy and convicted of perjury.

been scrutinized," and he called McCarthy "way off-base."[9] The two men had a brawl in a Washington, D.C., restaurant, which apparently started with McCarthy saying to Pearson, "I'm going to tear you limb from limb."[10] Soon McCarthy went after Pearson in earnest, trying to discredit him.

On December 15, 1950, McCarthy made an emotional speech to Congress that was filled with innuendos and few facts, claiming that Pearson was "a Moscow-directed character assassin"[11] and calling for a patriotic boycott of his radio show. Pearson in turn filed a $5.1 million libel suit against the senator, which was later dropped. McCarthy's accusations caused Pearson to lose radio sponsors, and many newspapers dropped his syndicated column. Few came out to support Pearson. The ominous truth was apparent: If McCarthy could silence a popular critic like Pearson by unsubstantiated smears, then no one was safe.

McCarthy both amazed and horrified people, who could do little more than watch him blaze across the headlines. A *Time* magazine reporter wrote, "'Man is born to do something,' says restless Joe McCarthy. Joe is doing something. His name is in headlines. 'McCarthyism' is now part of the language. His burly figure casts its shadow over the coming presidential campaign. Thousands turn out to hear his speeches. Millions regard him as 'a splendid American' (a fellow Senator recently called him that). Other millions think McCarthy a worse menace than the Communist conspiracy against which he professes to fight."[12]

McCarthy pushed the boundaries of the law and the Constitution to achieve his ends, but he was not alone. The FBI, local police, and other groups were also intent on snaring alleged Communists. In the early 1950s, the FBI passed the names of state employees suspected of being subversive to governors around the country. Without the opportunity to defend themselves against the accusations, hundreds of college professors, schoolteachers, and state workers lost their jobs. Many people were horrified at what was happening. Even President Truman was uncomfortable with this willingness to ignore the rules of fair play. On August 14, 1951, he spoke at the new American Legion building in Washington, D.C. In this important speech, carried on nationwide broadcast, Truman warned against the danger of trampling on freedom in the name of fighting Communism.

. . . Americanism is under attack by communism, at home and abroad. We are defending it against that attack. And we are protecting our country from spies and saboteurs. We are breaking up the Communist conspiracy in the United States. We are building our defenses, and making our country strong, and helping our allies to help themselves. If we keep on doing these things—if we put our best into the job—we can protect ourselves from the attack of communism.

But Americanism is also under another kind of attack. It is being undermined by some people in this country who are loudly proclaiming that they are its chief defenders. These people claim to be against communism. But they are chipping away at our basic freedoms just as insidiously and far more effectively than the Communists have ever been able to do. These people have attacked our basic principle of fair play that underlies our Constitution. They are trying to create fear and suspicion among us by the use of slander, unproved accusations, and just plain lies. . . .[13]

Conspiracy to Commit Espionage

While Senator McCarthy was fanning the anti-Communist flames in Washington, D.C., in New York City, the headlines were about a previously unknown couple, arrested just after the start of the Korean War for allegedly spying for the Soviet Union. Julius and Ethel Rosenberg were Communist Party members who had been accused of passing secrets about the making of the atomic bomb to the Soviets. Though they maintained their innocence, and the evidence against them was thin, there was little public sympathy for anyone suspected of espionage during the height of the Cold War and the Korean War. All the same, the Rosenbergs had supporters around the world who believed them to be innocent victims of the Red Scare, framed because they were Communists, the children of immigrants, and Jewish.

SPIES OR VICTIMS?

Julius Rosenberg was born in New York City in 1918 to poor Jewish immigrants who worked in garment sweatshops on the Lower East Side. He became a leader in the Young Communist League USA, the youth arm of the Communist Party USA. This is where he met his future wife, Ethel, the daughter of a Russian immigrant who had a sewing machine repair shop. Ethel was a clerk and a sometime labor activist who was three years younger than Julius. Julius graduated with a degree in electrical engineering from the City College of New York in 1939. The couple married, and, in 1940, he joined the Army Signal Corps as a civilian engineer, assigned to work on radar equipment. In 1945, he was fired because he had lied about his membership in the Communist Party. The couple had two sons, Robert and Michael.

On July 18, 1950, Julius was arrested at the family's small eleventh-floor apartment on the Lower East Side and taken to FBI headquarters in Foley Square on suspicion of spying for the Soviet Union. He was accused of being part of a complicated spy ring that spanned from the United States to England and the Soviet Union. Months earlier, a German-born physicist named Klaus Emil Fuchs, living in London, had confessed to passing British and American nuclear secrets to the Soviets. Fuchs had worked for the Manhattan Project in Los Alamos, New Mexico, during World War II. The Manhattan Project was a top-secret government effort to build the atomic bomb. Fuchs was arrested in London, and, in January 1950, he admitted handing information about the development of the hydrogen bomb, as well as other nuclear information, to Soviet agents. Fuchs was sentenced to 14 years in prison.

Fuchs's confession led to the arrest of Harry Gold, a Swiss-born Philadelphia chemist who was thought to be the courier for the spy ring. Soon after, Ethel Rosenberg's brother, David Greenglass, was arrested for his alleged involvement. Greenglass had worked for the Manhattan Project, designing models of bomb parts, including parts for the plutonium bomb, the type later dropped on Nagasaki, Japan, to end World War II. In his confession, Greenglass told the authorities that his brother-in-law Julius Rosenberg had recruited him to spy for the Soviets. Greenglass told prosecutors that he provided information on nuclear weapons to Julius. Julius said he passed the information to Gold, who turned it over to the Soviet Union's vice consul in New York, a man named Anatoly A. Yakovlev. On August 11, FBI director J. Edgar Hoover ordered that Ethel also be arrested. He thought her arrest might provide enough leverage to make Julius confess. Greenglass said that his sister had typed notes for him that contained nuclear secrets.

THE TRIAL

After months of preparation, the trial began on March 6, 1951, in the federal courthouse in New York. The Rosenbergs and their codefendant, an electrical engineer named Morton Sobell, were defended by the father and son lawyers Alexander and Emanuel Bloch, who often defended leftist causes. They faced a high-profile prosecution team determined to defeat Communism. The chief prosecutor, Irving Saypol, was already famous for prosecuting Alger Hiss. One of his assistants was Roy Cohn, a well-known anti-Communist who would serve as McCarthy's chief lawyer at the 1953 Army-McCarthy hearings. Cohn had recently prosecuted William Walter Remington, an economist accused of being a Soviet spy.

In his opening statement, prosecutor Saypol said, "The evidence will show that the loyalty and the allegiance of the Rosenbergs and Sobell were not to our country, but that it was to Communism, Communism in this country and throughout the world."[1] Saypol continued, ". . . the evidence will show that these defendants joined with their co-conspirators in a deliberate, carefully planned conspiracy to deliver to the Soviet Union the information and the weapons the Soviet Union could use to destroy us."[2] He implied that they had

Fear of Communism and Soviet spies spiked during the trial of Ethel and Julius Rosenberg (*above*), two American citizens accused and convicted of conspiracy to commit espionage.

committed treason, though that was not what they were charged with; nevertheless, the odds for the Rosenbergs being found innocent seemed very small.

Greenglass, who was being tried separately, was the chief witness for the prosecution. Greenglass gave many incriminating details about Julius's activities, including him cutting a Jell-O box in two to use as a signal in spy activities. He said that Rosenberg offered him money and a plan for them to escape to the Soviet Union. Greenglass's wife, Ruth, who had also been arrested but was not indicted, said that Julius had requested her to ask her husband at Los Alamos to help pass information to the Soviets. She also told the jury that she had seen Ethel typing David Greenglass's handwritten notes from Los Alamos. The Greenglasses' testimony ensured that David would avoid the death penalty.

Other witnesses included Elizabeth Bentley, a known ex-Soviet spy who had become an informer and even wrote books about her spy years. The notorious Bentley, nicknamed the Red Spy Queen, testified that she had connected Rosenberg with Jacob Golos, chief of the KGB's American operations. The KGB was the Soviets' national security agency. She said that she received several phone calls from someone who identified himself as "Julius" asking to talk with Golos.

The Rosenbergs were the only two witnesses for the defense. They volunteered to testify, even though they didn't have to do so. When asked if they were members of the Communist Party, they pleaded the Fifth Amendment, which protects witnesses from having to incriminate themselves. However, they did answer other questions, which they would have avoided had they not taken the stand. Julius was asked about past friendships, whether he believed the Soviet economic system was better than America's, and if he would fight to defend his country. He attempted to show that he was loyal to the United States, but the jury apparently was skeptical.

The evidence against Ethel was negligible and rested mostly on Ruth Greenglass's testimony, but the prosecution painted a picture of a home-based spy effort of which she was a part, including the typing incident. Ethel was only five feet (152 centimeters) tall and weighed 100 pounds (45 kilograms). She was the mother of two young children. Though Ethel might have gotten sympathy from the jury if she had portrayed herself as a victim of mistaken loyalty to her husband, she did not do so. In her testimony, she stood behind Julius. Nor did she conceal her contempt for the proceedings. A last-minute witness for the prosecution, a passport photographer who said he took the

Rosenbergs' passport pictures, helped to clinch the case. The prosecution put him on at the end of the trial to support the idea that the Rosenbergs wanted passport photos in order to flee to the Soviet Union; however, he had no negatives or business records to confirm his story.

In his summation, the Rosenbergs' attorney Emanuel Bloch tried to appeal to emotion to gain sympathy for Ethel. He labeled David Greenglass's testimony against his sister as "repulsive" and "a violation of every code that civilization has ever lived by. He is the lowest of the lowest animals that I have ever seen."[3] In his summation for the prosecution, Saypol said that the defendants' Communist ideology had led them to worship the Soviet Union. "These defendants before you are party to an agreement to spy and steal from their own country, to serve the interests of a foreign power which today seeks to wipe us off the face of the earth. . . . No defendants ever stood before the bar of American justice less deserving of sympathy than these three."[4] He also said the defendants worshipped Communism, which gave them the motive to do these terrible things.

DEATH SENTENCE

The jury took less than a day to deliberate. On March 29, the jury found the Rosenbergs and Sobell guilty of conspiracy to commit espionage by stealing atomic bomb secrets for the Soviet Union during wartime. Federal judge Irving R. Kaufman showed no mercy on April 5, when he imposed death sentences on both Julius and Ethel. Calling their crime "worse than murder," he said that they were in part responsible for the Korean War: "Putting into the hands of the Russians the A-bomb years before our best scientists predicted Russia would perfect the bomb has already caused, in my opinion, the Communist aggression in Korea, with the resultant casualties exceeding 50,000 and who knows but what that millions more innocent people may pay the price for your treason. Indeed, by your betrayal, you undoubtedly have altered the course of history to the disadvantage of our country."[5] He called Ethel a full-fledged partner in the crime. Shocked by the double death sentence, attorney Emanuel Bloch continued to declare their innocence to reporters. "I repeat that these defendants assert their innocence and will continue to assert it as long as they breathe. They believe that they are victims of political hysteria, and that their sentences were based upon extraneous political considerations having no legitimate or legal connection with the crime charged against them," he said in a report on the verdict in the *New York Times*.[6]

The Rosenbergs were sentenced to death under the Espionage Act of 1917, passed during the First Red Scare. Morton Sobell was sentenced to 30 years in prison and served nearly 19 years. Greenglass was given a 15-year sentence and served 10 years. When asked years later if he regretted informing on his sister and brother-in-law, Greenglass said that he didn't because he was protecting his wife and children.

EXECUTIONS

For two years, the Rosenbergs' lawyers fruitlessly tried to get the verdict of the case overturned. They appealed to the U.S. Supreme Court nine times, but the Court refused to review the case. The Rosenbergs tried to get both President Harry Truman and later President Dwight D. Eisenhower to grant clemency, but their efforts were to no avail. The verdict held. The two never admitted guilt, declaring their innocence until the end. Saying that they would be vindicated by history, Ethel called herself and her husband the first victims of American Fascism.

Julius and Ethel Rosenberg were executed by the electric chair at Sing Sing prison in Ossining, New York, on June 19, 1953. They were the first U.S. civilians executed for espionage. Ethel Rosenberg was the first woman executed by federal government in the United States since Mary Surratt was hanged in 1865 for conspiring to kill Abraham Lincoln. To many, the

(continues on page 60)

THE LAST LETTER

From their cells in Sing Sing prison, Ethel and Julius Rosenberg hoped that a storm of public protest might help get them a new trial. Outside the prison, support for the Rosenbergs grew as the *National Guardian*, a weekly left-wing New York newspaper, published a series of articles maintaining that the Rosenbergs were victims of the Cold War and a Communist witch hunt. The National Committee to Secure Justice in the Rosenberg Case was formed to keep the couple alive, but many were afraid to publicly support the couple. Though members privately expressed admiration, the American Communist Party did not take a public stand for the Rosenbergs. Jewish organizations kept their distance, declaring that Communism and Judaism are not compatible.

Meanwhile, in prison the couple maintained their innocence and tried to keep up their hope. They wrote more than 500 letters to their attorneys, each other, their sons, and others. As they appealed their case as far up as the U.S. Supreme Court, both Ethel and Julius were defiant and denied their guilt. Their last letter to their sons was dated the day of their execution.

June 19, 1953
Dearest Sweethearts, my most precious children,
Only this morning it looked like we might be together again after all. Now that this cannot be, I want so much for you to know all that I have come to know. Unfortunately, I may write only a few simple words; the rest your own lives must teach you, even as mine taught me.

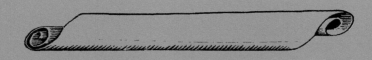

At first, of course, you will grieve bitterly for us, but you will not grieve alone. That is our consolation and it must eventually be yours.

Eventually, too you must come to believe that life is worth the living. Be comforted that even now, with the end of ours slowly approaching, that we know this with a conviction that defeats the executioner!

Your lives must teach you, too, that good cannot really flourish in the midst of evil; that freedom and all the things that go to make up a truly satisfying and worthwhile life, must sometimes be purchased very dearly. Be comforted then that we were serene and understood with the deepest kind of understanding, that civilization had not as yet progressed to the point where life did not have to be lost for the sake of life; and that we were comforted in the sure knowledge that others would carry on after us.

We wish we might have had the tremendous joy and gratification of living our lives out with you. Your Daddy who is with me in these last momentous hours, sends his heart and all the love that is in it for his dearest boys. Always remember that we were innocent and could not wrong our conscience.

We press you close and kiss you with all our strength.

Lovingly,
DADDY AND MOMMY
JULIE AND ETHEL

"The Rosenbergs' Last Letter," The Rosenberg Fund for Children. http://www.rfc.org/lastletter.

After they were convicted of conspiring to commit espionage, the Rosenbergs were sentenced to die by electric chair. Many believed that the death penalty was too severe, but their protests and appeals were ignored, and the Rosenbergs were executed in 1953.

(continued from page 57)

death penalty seemed excessive. After all, others convicted of similar crimes, including Fuchs, who was a key person in the spy ring, and Alger Hiss, a high-ranking federal employee, only got prison sentences.

The Rosenberg sons, Robert and Michael, were ages 6 and 10 at the time. After their parents' execution, the boys were adopted by their parents' friends, the Meeropols, and took that name. Michael became an economics professor, and Robert became an anthropologist and later a lawyer. For decades, the two sons tried to prove their parents' innocence. In the 1970s, they sued the federal government under the Freedom of Information Act, finally winning the release of 300,000 secret documents relating to their parents' case, in hopes of proving their innocence.

NEW EVIDENCE OF GUILT

The FBI's J. Edgar Hoover famously called the Rosenbergs' deeds the "crime of the century,"[7] but for the next half century the couple's guilt was hotly debated. Many people felt they were victims of overzealous prosecutors, using cooked-up evidence, during the Second Red Scare, and that the prosecution had framed them. Critics wondered if anyone accused of aiding Communism at a time when both the Cold War and the Korean War were raging could get a fair trial. Others thought they were guilty, but that the two death sentences were excessive; still others thought the death penalty was appropriate.

The answers to some of the questions began to come in the 1990s. After the fall of Communism in the Soviet Union, the Soviets opened old KGB files that revealed Julius Rosenberg was most likely a spy, though Ethel's role was not apparent. Later, on September 11, 2008, the transcript with testimony of 43 of the witnesses who appeared in front of the grand jury investigating the Rosenbergs before their trial was made public and it revealed more information. Also that day, during an interview on CBS, David Greenglass confessed that he had committed perjury during the trial in order to avoid the death penalty. Under pressure from the prosecution, he said, he had lied to the court that Ethel had typed his reports to Moscow: "I don't know who typed it, frankly, and to this day I can't remember that the typing took place. I had no memory of that at all—none whatsoever."[8] He said that he had done so to protect himself and his wife, at the urging of the prosecution. Although Greenglass said that he was sorry that his sister and brother-in-law had been put to death, he would not apologize for what he did. He said, "I would not sacrifice my wife and my children for my sister."[9]

In 2008, more information emerged suggesting that Julius Rosenberg did pass information to the Soviets, though not about the atomic bomb. In an interview with *New York Times* reporter Sam Roberts, the Rosenbergs' codefendant Morton Sobell, then 91 years old, admitted that he, himself, was a Soviet spy. At that point, even the Rosenbergs' sons conceded that Julius Rosenberg was most likely a spy, and that Ethel was knowledgeable about his actions but did not participate. However, the question of whether the death penalty was warranted is another matter.

The Rosenberg children were left to pick up the pieces. In 1990, son Robert started the Rosenberg Fund for Children, a foundation to help children of parents who had been accused of political crimes. In an interview, he discussed his response to the last letter of his parents: "My parents' last letter to me and my brother stands out for me. They wrote that they died secure in the knowledge that others would carry on after them. And I think that has multiple meanings. I think it meant, on a personal level to me and my brother, that other people would take care of us after they were no longer able to do so. But I also think it meant on the political level their political beliefs, the principles that they stood up for, their refusal to lie, their refusal to be pawns of the McCarthyite hysteria, in other words their refusal to be used to attack the movements that they believed in—that even though they were no longer able to carry on those struggles, others would be able to carry them on their absence. And I saw that as a call for me to do the same."[10]

ON THE OFFENSIVE

The Rosenbergs' trial and execution only heightened the anti-Communist hysteria. In 1953, the Cincinnati Reds baseball team changed its name to the Cincinnati Redlegs, to avoid having the baseball players investigated for subversion. Children's books, including *The Adventures of Robin Hood*, with its so-called "radical" message of robbing from the rich and giving to the poor, were pulled off the shelves of public libraries. The anti-Communist hysteria had gripped the nation, and McCarthy was on the offensive.

McCarthy criticized leaders in the government, lambasting Secretary of State Dean Acheson for his foreign policy with Moscow. He attacked General George C. Marshall, the chief of staff of the U.S. Army in World War II and secretary of state under President Truman. Truman had sent Marshall to negotiate peace between nationalist leader Chiang Kai-shek and Mao Tse-tung, leader of the Communists, during the Chinese civil war in 1947. When both leaders refused to cooperate, he withdrew American support from Chiang Kai-shek, which many people believed led to Mao's Communist victory, a serious blow to the United States. McCarthy went further than most critics of that move, however; he held nothing back when he attacked Marshall on the floor of the Senate in June 1951. He accused him of being part of a Communist conspiracy, a charge that shocked many and led McCarthy's supporters to doubt him. But even his Republican colleagues were unable to stop him. Senator Robert Taft, a leader of the Republican Party, said to a friend that it was impossible to rein him in: "You are mistaken when you suggest I have influence on McCarthy."[11]

The Army-McCarthy Hearings

As McCarthy began his second term in office in 1953, he was full of confidence. His sense of purpose and the certainty of his own importance were strong. He felt the fate of the nation was on his shoulders and that everything he did or said was terribly significant and always right. Yet his flame was starting to sputter, and his dominance of the daily headlines was about to fade. McCarthy was oblivious, or didn't much care, about the growing animosity toward him. During a historical congressional hearing, where the tables were finally turned and he was one of those being investigated, McCarthy would continue to bully witnesses, berate his enemies, and boast about his own significance. "This Committee's activities may well determine whether this nation will live or die!"[1] declared McCarthy during the Army-McCarthy hearings, which would wind up setting his fate on a downward spiral.

McCarthy had won reelection to the Senate in November 1952, with 54 percent of the Wisconsin vote. For the first time in 20 years, a Republican had captured the White House. President Dwight D. Eisenhower, a five-star general who led the Allied forces to victory in World War II, was inaugurated in January 1953, along with Vice President Richard Nixon. Nixon had made anti-Communism a major issue on the campaign trail, accusing Truman and his democratic predecessor, Franklin D. Roosevelt, of allowing the Communist conspiracy to grow. The Republicans—along with McCarthy—now possessed powerful sway in both Congress and the executive branch of the government. President Eisenhower was a moderate Republican who personally disliked McCarthy and did not approve of what many were now calling the Communist witch hunts. However, in the climate of fear and paranoia fraught by the Cold War, President Eisenhower did not take a strong stand against him at first. Eisenhower felt that he couldn't publicly chastise McCarthy, fearing that he, too, could be tarnished, though he did so in private conversations—and let Vice President Nixon do it in public.

In his new term, McCarthy was made chairman of the Senate Committee on Government Operations, which included the Senate Permanent Subcommittee on Investigations, charged with investigating corruption in government and civil service. He hired the conservative New York attorney Roy Cohn, who had helped prosecute the Rosenbergs, as counsel for the subcommittee, and Robert F. Kennedy as assistant counsel. The young Kennedy got along well with McCarthy at first, but he did not like Cohn, who would become the brains behind McCarthy's mounting anti-Communist crusade. The two would wind up clashing, as McCarthy used his subcommittee as a high-profile vehicle to launch fresh attacks, sometimes on the basis of the flimsiest of evidence.

Between 1953 and 1954, McCarthy's subcommittee interrogated nearly 400 people in closed-door sessions, including such cultural icons as the poet Langston Hughes and mystery writer Dashiell Hammett. On March 24, Cohn interrogated Hammett, author of *The Maltese Falcon* and other popular hard-boiled detective stories for books and films:

> Q. Are you a member of the Communist Party today?
>
> A. I decline to answer on the ground that the answer would tend to incriminate me, pleading my rights under the Fifth Amendment.
>
> Q. Were you a member of the Communist Party in 1922?
>
> A. I decline to answer on the ground that the answer might tend to incriminate me.
>
> Q. You have written a number of books between 1922 and the present time, have you not?
>
> A. Yes.
>
> Q. About how many?
>
> A. Five, I think.
>
> Q. Just five books?
>
> A. Yes, and many short stories and stuff that has been reprinted in reprint books.
>
> Q. If I were to ask you as to each one of these books if you were a Communist Party member at the time you wrote the book what would your answer be?[2]

NEW ATTACKS

The new Republican majority in Washington had changed the landscape, but McCarthy did not relent on his crusade to uncover Communists in government. Now when McCarthy bombarded the government with accusations of being soft on Communism, he was attacking his fellow Republicans, a perilous move for a senator. One of his targets was the Voice of America (VOA), an international broadcasting service operated by the United States Information Agency (USIA), a federal agency. The VOA radio broadcasts about news, culture, and information from the United States were heard around

When McCarthy attacked the U.S. Army for not investigating the possible Communist presence at Fort Monmouth, New Jersey, the army retaliated and accused McCarthy of seeking special privileges for friends. These hearings (*above*) were nationally televised, allowing the American public to see Senator McCarthy live for the first time. Seated from left to right: Army secretary Robert Stevens, Major General Robert Young, Roy Cohn, and McCarthy.

the world. Some Communist countries even tried to block VOA broadcasts. But amid the anti-Communist climate of the early 1950s, within the VOA there was disagreement over its mission: Should the VOA just report the news or should it use its radio broadcasts to fight Communism? Employees who just wanted to report the news became suspect. When rumors of Communists and corruption in the VOA began spreading, McCarthy decided to investigate.

On February 16, 1953, the subcommittee hearings opened at a New York City courthouse. McCarthy began his attack, questioning the loyalty of some employees and the competence of others. He read aloud the poor college grades of one of the engineers. Employees of VOA were brought before the subcommittee and accused of Communist sympathies. One employee was humiliated for not believing in God; another was suspect because he did not want to do another broadcast on Abraham Lincoln. One VOA employee subsequently committed suicide, leaving a note to his family that said he had done nothing "which I did not think was in the best interests of this country."[3] None were found guilty.

After the VOA hearings ended inconclusively, McCarthy quickly picked a new target—the Overseas Library Program run by the USIA. He sent Cohn and his young aide G. David Schine to investigate State Department libraries around Europe. Books in these libraries had been selected by leading publishers and by professors at Harvard University. McCarthy was concerned that some of the books were pro-Communist or written by Communist sympathizers, such as Hammett's *The Maltese Falcon*. He held hearings, calling up dozens of writers. Most of them had no idea that their books were in the overseas library. Many of the witnesses took the Fifth Amendment and refused to answer questions about their political beliefs. The result of the hearings was chaos and disarray in the USIA.

THE HEARINGS

In the fall of 1953, McCarthy found a fresh, but dangerous, new focus—the U.S. Army. His subcommittee had been investigating a secret army research facility at Fort Monmouth, a large army base in New Jersey. An army dentist named Irving Peress at the base was suspected of being a security risk, but the army had still promoted him to major. In fact, Peress, a dentist from

Queens, New York, was a member of the Communist Party, but historians now believe it is doubtful that as an army dentist he posed any sort of security threat. However, Julius Rosenberg had also worked at Fort Monmouth during World War II. In McCarthy's view, Peress's promotion and the Rosenberg connection at Fort Monmouth cast a cloud of suspicion on the entire army.

The Eisenhower administration and the army lobbied back with accusations of their own against McCarthy and his staff. Cohn's young friend, G. David Schine, was an unpaid consultant on the subcommittee. The wealthy son of a hotel chain owner, Schine was a Harvard University graduate and an anti-Communist. In early 1953, he accompanied Cohn around Europe to investigate the libraries in Europe. Then in November 1953, Schine was drafted into the army. According to the army, Cohn tried to get his friend preferential treatment so that he would not have to do the duties of an ordinary army private. Cohn's requests, which eventually went as far as the secretary of the army, backfired. The Eisenhower administration accused McCarthy and his staff of seeking favors and special privileges for Schine. McCarthy turned the tables and charged the army with using the Schine case to stop his investigations into the Communist infiltration of the army.

McCarthy's subcommittee had to hold hearings on these matters. Since McCarthy was part of the inquiry, he was forced to step down as the chairman. Instead of hiring himself a lawyer, McCarthy chose to represent himself, which was probably a mistake. Now McCarthy was on full public display.

The minority leader of the Senate, Lyndon Johnson, a democrat from Texas and a future U.S. president, disliked McCarthy. Johnson urged that the hearings be televised. So when the Army-McCarthy hearings began on April 22, 1954, in the Senate Caucus Room at Capitol Hill, the television cameras were rolling. Most important, the hearings were broadcast live,

(continues on page 72)

EDWARD R. MURROW

Television viewers tuning in to the CBS news show *See It Now* on March 9, 1954, saw a special investigation titled "A Report on Senator Joseph McCarthy." Broadcast journalist Edward R. Murrow, who had gained fame with his radio broadcasts from Europe during World War II, vigorously attacked McCarthy on national television. Finally, someone had dared to take on McCarthy, unafraid for their own job or reputation. Viewed under an unflattering spotlight on national television, the end was near for the Wisconsin senator.

The handsome, dark-haired Murrow was a pioneer of broadcast journalism, known for his independence and fierce integrity. He was born Egbert Roscoe Murrow in 1908 to a Quaker family in North Carolina. His father was a tenant farmer who moved the family to Washington State, where Murrow worked as a teenager in logging camps during the summers. After graduating from Washington State College, where he had his own radio show, he moved to New York City, where he became president of the National Student Federation. In 1935, he was hired by the broadcasting company CBS to help publicize the educational uses for radio.

Murrow was working for CBS in London when the war broke out. To cover the war as it unfolded, Murrow directed a team of reporters for CBS in Europe. His gravely intelligent war commentary on the radio became renowned, particularly when he reported on Germany's air raids on London. "This . . . is London," he would say to open each broadcast. In terse, poetic language, Murrow described the gritty scenes of war, as he saw them. He also flew 25 missions with Allied pilots, reporting from the air. When Murrow witnessed the liberation of the Nazi concentration camp at Buchenwald in April 1945, he was overcome by the sight of both the dead and the starving survivors with numbers stamped on their arms. In his broadcast

three days later, Murrow expressed his horror, "I pray you to believe what I have said about Buchenwald. I reported what I saw and heard, but only part of it. For most of it, I have no words. If I have offended you by this rather mild account of Buchenwald, I'm not in the least sorry. . . ."*

Murrow returned to New York and moved into the new medium of television. Starting in 1951, he did news documentaries for the weekly CBS program *See It Now*. In 1953, Murrow turned his attention to McCarthyism. He decided to investigate the case of Milo Radulovich, who had been discharged from the U.S. Air Force because his mother and sister were Communist sympathizers. In his report, Murrow criticized the air force's decision; the result was that Radulovich was reinstated in the air force. When Murrow learned McCarthy was preparing to attack him personally, the newsman gathered up information he had collected over several years and prepared a special 30-minute report on the senator.

The report was expected to be so controversial that CBS did not give its full approval, making Murrow and his producer Fred Friendly pay for newspaper advertisements to promote the show. In fact, the show on March 9 was mostly a compilation of McCarthy's own words, which Murrow highlighted to show both his hypocrisy and fanaticism. McCarthy twisted facts and changed his accusations to fit the circumstances. Murrow ended the broadcast with this famous comment, reflecting on both McCarthy and the public who had been willing to follow him:

> We must not confuse dissent with disloyalty. We must remember always that accusation is not proof and that conviction depends

(continues)

(continued)

upon evidence and due process of law. . . . We will not walk in fear, one of another. We will not be driven by fear into an age of unreason. If we dig deep in our history and doctrine, and remember, we are not descended from fearful men. Not from men who feared to write, to speak, to associate, and to defend the causes that were for the moment unpopular. . . . The actions of the junior senator from Wisconsin have caused alarm and dismay to our allies abroad and given considerable comfort to our enemies. And whose fault is that? Not really his. He didn't create the situation of fear—he merely exploited it. And rather successfully. Cassius was right. "The fault, Dear Brutus, is not in our stars, but in ourselves. . . .**

As he always did, Murrow ended the broadcast with his trademark farewell, "Good night, and good luck." The public reaction to the *See It Now* special on McCarthy was overwhelming. Thousands of telegrams, phone calls, and letters poured into CBS offices, almost all in favor of the show. McCarthy tried to fight back. On a radio broad-

(continued from page 69)
a revolutionary occurrence since television was a relatively new medium. Two channels, ABC and DuMont television network, which is now defunct, carried the hearings' full schedule of 188 hours. CBS and NBC carried the first day live and then reported on the hearings on the nightly news.

Across the country, people gathered around televisions as the hearings played out in the spring of 1954. Some 20 million people are estimated to have tuned in. For most, this was their

cast, he called Murrow an "extreme left-wing bleeding heart."*** He was invited to appear on *See It Now* to respond three weeks later, but on live TV without an audience, he performed poorly and failed to reverse the tide building against him. Murrow's broadcasts are now considered to have helped lead to McCarthy's downfall.

Despite CBS's reluctance to continue backing Murrow and his controversial reporting, *See It Now* stayed on the air until 1958. Before moving on from television, Murrow narrated the groundbreaking CBS documentary *Harvest of Shame* about the harsh lives of migrant farm workers in Florida, which aired just after Thanksgiving in 1960. Viewers were shocked to learn how the migrants suffered. A chain smoker who often smoked on camera, Murrow died of lung disease on April 27, 1965.

---

* "Edward R. Murrow's Report from Buchenwald," Jewish Virtual Library. http://www.jewishvirtuallibrary.org/jsource/Holocaust/murrow.html.
** Text of *See It Now* (March 9, 1954), hosted by University of Maryland at College Park. http://honors.umd.edu/HONR269J/archive/Murrow5403 09.html.
*** Arthur Herman, *Joseph McCarthy: Reexamining the Life and Legacy of America's Most Hated Senator.* New York: The Free Press, 2000, p. 254.

first glimpse of Senator McCarthy in action—and the experience was not a positive one. He frequently interrupted the people being questioned, trying to insert himself into the hearings. *New York Times* reporter James Reston wrote that "the senator from Wisconsin is a bad-tempered man" who was hurting himself by his "manner and manners."[4] His bullying tactics, magnified on camera, turned many people off.

McCarthy attacked Robert T. Stevens, the secretary of the army, and General Ralph Zwicker for not suitably investigating suspected espionage at Fort Monmouth. He held nothing back when he grilled General Zwicker about giving Peress an honorable discharge:

> McCarthy: Did you know that [Peress] refused to answer questions about his Communist activity?
>
> Zwicker: Specifically, I don't believe so.
>
> McCarthy: Did you have any idea?
>
> Zwicker: Of course I had an idea.
>
> McCarthy: What do you think he was called down here for?
>
> Zwicker: For that specific purpose.
>
> McCarthy: Then you knew that those were the questions he was asked, did you not? General, let's try and be truthful. I am going to keep you here as long as you keep hedging and hemming.
>
> Zwicker: I am not hedging.
>
> McCarthy: Or hawing.
>
> Zwicker: I am not hawing, and I don't like to have anyone impugn my honesty, which you just about did.
>
> (and later)
>
> McCarthy: Then, general, you should be removed from any command. Any man who has been given the honor of being promoted to general and who says, "I will protect another general who protected Communists," is not fit to wear that uniform.[5]

McCarthy had stepped over the line. Zwicker was a war hero in World War II, and for McCarthy to say that he was unfit to wear a uniform was outrageous to many, including President Eisenhower. The *New York Post* wrote in an editorial, "General Zwicker endured McCarthy's vilest abuses to uphold the fortress of executive authority in the Pentagon."[6] Further testimony also damaged McCarthy and his staff. While Cohn accused the army of holding Schine as blackmail to stop McCarthy from investigating subversives at Fort Monmouth, the army lawyer John G. Adams testified that Cohn had threatened to destroy the army.

McCarthy never looked worse than when he tried to smear a young lawyer who worked with Joseph N. Welch, the head counsel for the Eisenhower administration and the secretary of the army. McCarthy accused the young attorney Fred Fisher of being a member of the National Lawyers Guild, an organization for lawyers that was considered liberal, when he was a law student. In response, Welch responded with outrage, "Until this moment, Senator, I think I never really gauged your cruelty or your recklessness. Fred Fisher is a young man who went to the Harvard Law School and came into my firm and is starting what looks to be a brilliant career with us."[7] Fisher had told his boss that he belonged to the National Lawyers Guild at Harvard Law School, and Welch felt compelled to protect him. He sent Fisher back to Boston and out of the Washington limelight. He continued, "Let us not assassinate this lad further, Senator. You have done enough. Have you no sense of decency, sir, at long last? Have you left no sense of decency?"[8] Silence followed his remarks, as the weight of their meaning was felt by television viewers around the country.

AFTERMATH

The Army-McCarthy hearings lasted for 36 days, through the testimony of 32 witnesses. In the end, the committee concluded that McCarthy had not behaved improperly on behalf of G. David Schine. However, Cohn was found to have been unduly aggressive in support of his young friend, however. The committee also found the army had behaved questionably in its efforts to influence McCarthy's investigations at Fort Monmouth and to block subpoenas for witnesses by making personal appeals to McCarthy and his staff. Thus, neither side wound up looking very good. McCarthy had basically destroyed his reputation—and the army did not come off much better. Although McCarthy was not found to have committed any wrongdoing,

Cohn quit before he was fired. Then McCarthy's downfall began in earnest.

People began to be less frightened of speaking out against him. One cartoonist showed McCarthy hanging himself on a tree during the McCarthy hearings. Newspapers were more open about their criticism. Famous writers such as Walter Lippmann stepped up their open attacks on McCarthy. Republicans who had long held back their criticism became openly disdainful of their fellow senator. George N. Craig, the Republican governor of Indiana, told Eisenhower that he should discipline McCarthy to show that he will "not tolerate cheap headline hunting, self-aggrandizement, and bad manners" that imperil the Republican Party.[9] In April 1953, the popular Chicago bishop Bernard J. Sheil gave a passionate speech to a group of auto workers, breaking with the traditional Catholic support for McCarthy. The nation must "cry out against the phony anti-Communism that mocks our way of life, flouts our traditions and democratic procedures and our sense of fair play, feeds on the meat of suspicion and grows great on the dissension among Americans which it cynically creates and keeps alive by the mad pursuit of headlines,"[10] said Sheil. Few came to McCarthy's aid, as public approval of him fell sharply.

Still the era named for him was not over. Even as McCarthy's subcommittee's investigations were discontinued, the FBI and HUAC persisted in trying to hunt out Communists through the 1950s. One of their targets was the popular folk singer Pete Seeger. Born in 1919, Seeger was the son of a classical composer and music historian. During the 1930s, Seeger and his father traveled together through the South, collecting old folk songs for the Library of Congress's Archive of American Folk Song. Seeger was a talented musician. He played the guitar, banjo, and mandolin, and sang folk songs in a rough, gravelly voice that would become famous and known by many generations of music listeners.

Although there was a growing backlash against Senator McCarthy and his crusade, HUAC continued with their anti-Communist investigations. Folk musician Pete Seeger (*above*) was called to testify for his activities and was blacklisted until the 1960s.

In 1948, Seeger formed the Weavers, a popular folk music group that played favorite songs such as "On Top of Old Smoky" and "Goodnight Irene" in venues across the country. In the early 1950s, the Weavers were blacklisted and their record contract was cancelled. They could not find bookings. Seeger was called to Washington to testify before the HUAC in 1955. "I am not going to answer any questions as to my associations, my philosophical or my religious beliefs, or how I voted in any election or any of these private affairs. I think these are very improper questions for any American to be asked."[11] Seeger said.

He did not invoke the Fifth Amendment like others who refused to testify. When asked if he sang the song "If I Had a Hammer" at a rally for Communists on trial, Seeger replied, "I have sung for Americans of every political persuasion, and I am proud that I never refuse to sing to an audience, no matter what religion or color of their skin, or situation in life. I have sung in hobo jungles, and I have sung for the Rockefellers, and I am proud that I have never refused to sing for anybody."[12] Seeger was sentenced to a year in prison for contempt and was jailed briefly, but the verdict was reversed in 1962. Nevertheless, Seeger was on a network television blacklist until the late 1960s. After several rocky years, Seeger's career was revived and he flourished and became immensely popular during the folk revival of the 1960s.

Censure

McCarthy's attack on the young lawyer Fred Fisher at the Army-McCarthy hearings was the beginning of his downfall. After he was accused of being reckless and cruel by the government lawyer Joseph Welch, McCarthy continued to go after the National Lawyers Guild and Fisher. The audience in the room was shocked by McCarthy's rude behavior. Even McCarthy's friends and supporters saw that he had gone too far. "I was sick to my stomach,"[1] said one of McCarthy's former aides, Ray Kiermas, who sat in the audience. One Republican senator, Ralph Flanders, later wrote to a friend, "I cannot conceive of wanting to live, or wanting my children or grandchildren to live, in an America fashioned in the image of the junior senator from Wisconsin."[2]

In retrospect, historians agree that the Army-McCarthy hearings finished McCarthy's career and sealed his reputation.

(continues on page 82)

PAUL ROBESON

In 1949, a riot erupted at a Paul Robeson concert near Peekskill, New York. Robeson had been a popular singer and actor, with a stirring bass-baritone voice that was rich and full of emotion. He was also an avowed Communist. In the midst of the Cold War, the protestors did not want Robeson on stage or anywhere nearby. He barely escaped with his life.

Singing was one of Robeson's many talents. Born in New Jersey in 1898, his father had escaped slavery to become a Presbyterian minister. His mother was from a prominent Philadelphia family. A talented student, Robeson was the first African American to graduate from Rutgers University when he gave the valedictory address in 1919. Robeson was also a star athlete, winning 15 varsity letters in football and other sports. He went on to graduate from Columbia University Law School and began a career as an actor and singer. One of very few African Americans to be given leading roles, Robeson played Othello in a long-running Broadway production of the Shakespeare play. He used his magnificent voice to perform African-American spirituals and sing in films and Broadway musicals, including *Porgy and Bess*, and to speak out for peace and justice. In Europe and around the world, Robeson performed and gave speeches against racism and oppression.

Robeson refused to perform in segregated concert halls, and he appealed to President Harry Truman to put an end to lynching. Robeson was also a member of the Communist Party USA. He was against the Cold War and sympathetic to the Soviet Union. In 1934, Robeson visited the Soviet Union, where he embraced the ideas of socialism. He lived for a time in London and traveled in Africa, where he was shocked by the poverty and effects of colonialism. In 1937, he came back to the United States. Fed up with the stereotypi-

cal roles for him in Hollywood, he quit the industry and concentrated on singing.

By the late 1940s, the charismatic Robeson had become a controversial figure. The West Virginia Library Commission banned a children's biography of Robeson from the library shelves. He was also banned from television. Robeson caused a controversy at the Paris Peace Conference in 1949 when he said in a speech that African Americans shouldn't fight in the Korean War until they were free at home. That year, at his concert in Peekskill, angry protestors smashed the stage, set fire to chairs, threw rocks at cars, and attacked audience members. The U.S. State Department revoked Robeson's passport in 1950, ending his ability to earn a livelihood in Europe.

For many years, Robeson tried unsuccessfully to get his passport back. In 1956, after he refused to sign a statement that he was not a Communist, Robeson was called to testify before the House Un-American Activities Committee. He took the Fifth Amendment when asked if he was a Communist, but he spoke strongly against the racism he'd encountered in the United States and voiced support for the Soviet Union.

I am not being tried for whether I am a Communist, I am being tried for fighting for the rights of my people, who are still second-class citizens in this United States of America. My mother was born in your state, Mr. Walter, and my mother was a Quaker, and my ancestors in the time of Washington baked bread for George Washington's troops when they crossed the Delaware, and my own father was a slave. I stand here struggling for the rights of

(continues)

(continued)

my people to be full citizens in this country. And they are not. They are not in Mississippi. And they are not in Montgomery, Alabama. And they are not in Washington. They are nowhere, and that is why I am here today. You want to shut up every Negro who has the courage to stand up and fight for the rights of his people, for the rights of workers, and I have been on many a picket line for the steelworkers too. And that is why I am here today. . . . *

The Supreme Court decided in 1958 that a citizen's beliefs or affiliations should not prevent him or her from traveling with a U.S. passport. Although Robeson celebrated the decision that returned him his passport with a sold-out concert at Carnegie Hall, he soon left the country, performing in concerts in England and Australia. He was treated for severe depression in England. After returning to the United States in 1963, Robeson struggled with health problems, living quietly in Philadelphia until his death in 1976. For many years, history books virtually erased Robeson from memory. Only recently have Robeson's dignity, courage, and achievements, along with his controversial viewpoints, begun to be recognized again.

---

* "'You Are the Un-Americans, and You Ought to be Ashamed of Yourselves': Paul Robeson Appears Before HUAC." *History Matters.* http://historymatters.gmu.edu/d/6440/.

(continued from page 79)

Public sentiment was building against him, as well. The month before the hearings, in March 1954, President Eisenhower had gotten his vice president, Richard Nixon, to speak out against

McCarthy's tactics. A strong anti-Communist who had sat on HUAC, Nixon gave a radio and television address to the nation. Saying that the procedures for dealing with Communists must be fair and proper, Nixon said famously, "Well. I'll agree; they're a bunch of rats, but just remember this. When you go out to shoot rats, you have to shoot straight, because when you shoot wildly, it not only means that the rats may get away more easily, you make it easier on the rat, but you might hit someone else who's trying to shoot rats, too. And so we've got to be fair. . . . And when through carelessness, you lump the innocent and the guilty together, what you do is to give the guilty a chance to pull the cloak of innocence around themselves."[3]

McCarthy's star was fading. He had spent years crusading against Communism in America, with the backing of many people. Exploiting the public's fears, he had used his position to expose alleged Communists in government, education, the media, labor unions, the law, and other parts of society. Some of his accusations were based on facts, but many of his charges grew from innuendo and rumor and wound up destroying lives and careers. Now the tide turned against him. Americans were less willing to trust the senator or believe that any of his charges had merit. "McCarthy was his own worst enemy . . . ,"[4] writes journalist Tom Wicker. The newspapers that had helped in his rise to power by keeping him in the headlines now began to ignore him. Instead of covering his every statement, some reporters refused to even quote him. His balloon was deflating fast—and so was the anti-Communist crusade that he had fanned into a national frenzy.

IMPROPER CONDUCT

After McCarthy attacked the army and openly criticized the Eisenhower administration, even his fellow senators decided that he must be stopped. On July 30, 1954, Senator Flanders of Vermont introduced a resolution to censure McCarthy for acts of improper conduct. A longtime critic of McCarthy, Flanders had tired of putting up with him, but he wasn't the only one. The Senate appointed a select committee known as the Watkins Committee, chaired by Utah Republican senator Arthur Watkins, to undertake the censure. The Watkins Committee deliberated for less than a month, from August 31 until September 13. The Republicans preferred to make a deal with McCarthy, but he continued to be combative. On November 8, the full committee recommended that McCarthy be censured.

The man who had learned to box in college years earlier didn't go without a fight. On November 10, 1954, McCarthy stood on the Senate floor and lashed out at his critics. He accused the Watkins Committee of siding with Communism and catering to the *Daily Worker*, the CP newspaper. "When the Watkins committee announced its recommendation of censure, the Communists made no attempt to conceal their joy. The *Daily Worker*'s headline that day read, 'Throw the Bum Out' (that's me) . . . Its cry was primarily one of self-congratulation, of smug jubilation over the success of the Communists' own efforts to rebuke me,"[5] he said. He went on to say, "I regard as the most disturbing phenomenon in America today the fact that so many Americans still refuse to acknowledge the ability of Communists to persuade loyal Americans to do their work."[6] And McCarthy promised to "continue to serve the cause in which I have dedicated my life."[7]

McCarthy's efforts to fight the censure were to no avail. On December 2, 1954, the full Senate voted 67 to 22 to condemn McCarthy, stating that he "repeatedly abused the subcommittee and its members who were trying to carry out assigned duties, thereby obstructing the constitutional processes of the Senate, and that this conduct of the Senator from Wisconsin, Mr. McCarthy, is contrary to senatorial traditions and is hereby condemned."[8] All the Democrats and about half the Republicans had voted against him. The resolution against McCarthy cited his violation of Senate rules of conduct, not his anti-Communist crusade, specifically two instances: his contempt of a Senate subcommittee that investigated him in 1951 and 1952, and his disrespectful treatment of General Zwicker. The rebuke did not remove him from his committee posts, but McCarthy had lost something more important—the respect of his colleagues and his stature as a senator.

Signaling that voters were fed up with the more conservative Republicans, Democrats won a majority in Congress in the November elections in 1954. As a Republican, McCarthy was removed from the chairmanship of the Senate Permanent Investigating Subcommittee. No longer would he have a platform to continue his anti-Communist investigations. After the Senate's rebuke of McCarthy, the American Federation of Labor met for its annual convention in Los Angeles. The labor groups and McCarthy were archenemies. Yet, according to *Time* magazine, there was almost no mention of McCarthy at the conference. "McCarthy is dead. Why should we bother kicking the corpse?"[9] one delegate said.

CHANGING WORLD

Even though McCarthy had damaged his own crusade, making people more skeptical of the Red Threat, the general distrust of Communism had not gone away. Still, the world was starting to change. President Eisenhower had signed a truce in June 1953 to end the fighting in Korea. The Korean peninsula was left divided between North and South, Communism and democracy. There was no American victory; yet Eisenhower saw peace as a better alternative than war, even if it meant not defeating the Chinese-backed Communists. "Every gun that is fired, every warship launched, every rocket fired signifies a theft from those who hunger and are not fed, those who are cold and are not clothed . . . ,"[10] he said. Republicans in Congress criticized Eisenhower for being soft on Communism and not seeking outright victory, but the president stood firm. "The war is over. I hope my son is going to come home soon,"[11] he said. Though American soldiers have been stationed in the demili-

The death of Soviet leader Joseph Stalin brought Nikita Khrushchev into the spotlight of world politics. Khrushchev (*above, with President Eisenhower*) publicized and condemned many of Stalin's past excesses and murderous actions, causing many to drop out of the Communist Party in America.

tarized zone between the two countries ever since, the fighting had ended. American soldiers were no longer risking their lives on the battlefield against Communism.

Change was also occurring in the Soviet Union. Joseph Stalin, the powerful and repressive dictator who had led a regime of terror since the late 1920s, died in 1953. The new leader, Nikita Khrushchev, promised a more tolerant regime and a willingness to reach out to the democratic West. In 1956, Khrushchev gave his famous Secret Speech, which denounced Stalin's excesses, the purges that killed tens of thousands of people and caused the suffering of millions, and the persecution of the Jewish people. Many American Communists were shocked by the revelations—as well as by the Soviet army's brutal suppression of the Hungarian Revolution that same year—and quit the party. The blacklisted novelist Howard Fast, a longtime Communist who had served a three-month sentence for contempt of Congress after refusing to testify before the HUAC, was one of many who gave up on the Communist Party. "It was incredible and unbelievable to me that Khrushchev did not end his speech with the promise of reforms needed to guarantee that Stalin's crimes will not be repeated,"[12] he told the *New York Times* in February 1957. Membership in the Communist Party fell drastically, and its newspaper, the *Daily Worker*, ceased publication soon after. Though he did not bring significant changes, Khrushchev offered a more humane face of Communism and of the Soviet Union. He visited the United States in 1959. Still, a real thaw in the Cold War would take much longer.

Meanwhile, liberals in Congress felt that they must prove they were still strong anti-Communists, despite their treatment of McCarthy. In the midst of the Watkins Committee deliberations, in August 1954, Congress passed the Communist Control Act. "The Congress hereby finds and declares that the Communist Party of the United States, although purportedly a political party, is in fact an instrumentality of a conspiracy to overthrow the Government of the United States,"[13] the act stated. Congress had effectively outlawed the Communist Party; however, the act did not stand up legally and would not be enforced.

COINTELPRO

Important decisions by the Supreme Court in the late 1950s were critical to ending the abuses of the McCarthy era. In particular, the Court curtailed the broad reach of power that had been exercised by congressional committees. The justices defended the right of witnesses to invoke the Fifth Amendment in *Slochower v. Board of Education* in 1956. In *Yates v. United States* (1957) the convictions of 14 Communists were reversed. And in 1957, the Court ruled in *Watkins v. United States* that the HUAC couldn't punish uncooperative witnesses, as it had for more than a decade. Writing for the majority, Justice Earl Warren said, "The mere summoning of a witness and compelling him to testify, against his will, about his beliefs, expressions or associations is a measure of governmental interference. And when those forced revelations concern matters that are unorthodox, unpopular, or even hateful to the general public, the reaction in the life of the witness may be disastrous."[14]

Although the Second Red Scare was waning, anti-Communist investigations by the federal government had not ended. Instead, they continued beneath a fuller cloak of secrecy, under the lead of J. Edgar Hoover at the FBI. "Indeed, the activities of the FBI and other intelligence agencies escalated sharply,"[15] writes McCarthy era scholar Richard Fried. In 1956, the FBI under Hoover developed a program to disrupt the Communist Party that soon expanded to investigating a wide range of organizations suspected of being subversive or antigovernment. The Counter Intelligence Program, or COINTELPRO, was aimed at infiltrating and disrupting Communist organizations, women's rights groups, militant African-American organizations, Vietnam war protesters, and even the civil rights movement. COINTELPRO also tried to disrupt white hate groups such as the Ku Klux Klan.

The public knew little of the program until 1971, when a group of leftist radicals broke into an FBI office in Pennsylvania and passed information to news reporters. Gradually, through

Senator Frank Church (*above*) helmed the Church Committee, a congressional group organized to look into the overzealous practices of the CIA and FBI. The Church Committee discovered, and denounced, these two agencies for breaking the law during their investigations of American political groups.

a series of lawsuits and news investigations, and finally a congressional committee known as the Church Committee, after Senate leader Frank Church, COINTELPRO was fully revealed. The Church Committee found that the FBI program went far beyond FBI guidelines for investigations and violated constitutional guarantees of freedom of speech and association. The Church Committee's final report, released in 1976, stated:

"Many of the techniques used would be intolerable in a democratic society even if all the targets had been involved in violent activity, but COINTELPRO went far beyond that. The unexpressed major premise of the programs was that a law enforcement agency has the duty to do whatever is necessary to combat perceived threats to the existing social and political order."[16] The Church Committee also investigated the FBI's activities against unpopular political groups going back to World War I during the First Red Scare when they deported dissidents for their beliefs. The verdict was clear: "The American people need to be assured that never again will an agency of the government be permitted to conduct a secret war against those citizens it considers threats to the established order. Only a combination of legislative prohibition and Departmental control can guarantee that COINTELPRO will not happen again."[17]

END OF AN ERA

McCarthy had married Jean Kerr, one of his Senate aides, on September 29, 1953, at a ceremony at St. Matthew's Cathedral in Washington, D.C. She was 29 years old and faithfully attended his censure hearings. They adopted a baby girl, but their happiness was short-lived. After McCarthy was censured by his Senate colleagues, his friends noticed that he was drinking heavily and his health was failing. He was in and out of the hospital. He had lost the chairmanship of his committee, but he remained in the Senate. However, people no longer paid attention to what he said.

After a rapid decline in his health, McCarthy died on May 2, 1957, at Bethesda Naval Hospital. He was only 48 years old. The cause of death was liver disease, probably related to years of heavy drinking. McCarthy was given a High Requiem Mass at St. Matthew's Cathedral in Washington. Then an honor guard of U.S. Marines carried his body to Capitol Hill for a service in the Senate chamber. He was buried with his parents back at his childhood home of Appleton, Wisconsin. Robert F. Kennedy was one of the mourners at his graveside.

McCarthy's downfall, followed quickly by his early death, marked the end of an era. The House Un-American Activities Committee that had begun in 1938 changed its name in 1968 and was abolished in 1975. The House Judiciary Committee took over its responsibilities. Even in its waning days, the HUAC did not fail to raise controversy. In 1960, at a HUAC hearing in San Francisco, students raised their objections and police used fire hoses and clubs to break up riots.[18] A new age was beginning—one in which young people would not tolerate being targeted for their political beliefs, and journalists, activists, and eventually politicians, religious leaders, and many other Americans would not, either.

Can It
Happen Again?

Senator Joseph McCarthy, J. Edgar Hoover, and other anti-Communist crusaders succeeded in some ways in achieving what they had set out to do. Their charges against alleged Communists were frequently inaccurate and their methods crude, often trampling civil liberties. Yet they had latched on to a real fear and successfully exploited it, without much opposition, at least at first. The anti-Communist attacks of the 1940s and 1950s weakened the Communist movement in the United States and also pushed leftist and liberal groups and ideologies to the margins of society.

At the same time, the McCarthy era left bitterness and anger, and a determination that it should not happen again. The fears raised by McCarthy were clearly exaggerated. Though Communism posed a threat from outside the nation's borders during the Cold War, there was never a real danger that

American Communists could overthrow the government. In the end, McCarthyism became a synonym for smear tactics, unsubstantiated accusations, and mudslinging to ruin a person's reputation. McCarthy sought political power by playing on the public's anxiety. His loose regard for the truth, slandering of opponents as unpatriotic, use of innuendo and association to imply guilt, and strong-arm tactics that included terrorizing witnesses who came before his committee, appalled many people. Critics say that he did not worry whether his accusations were true, false, or somewhere in the muddy middle.

For these reasons, McCarthy remains a dark and controversial figure. "At his best, he produced evidence that the government's security procedures were sometimes remiss. But his critics were right: he never uncovered a Communist," writes David M. Oshinsky in *A Conspiracy So Immense*.[1] Others disagree. Some people believe that McCarthy was at least partially justified in his anti-Communist crusade and did succeed in stopping a menace. They point to recently disclosed classified information that shows he may have exaggerated the so-called Communist conspiracy, but some of it was real.

NEW INFORMATION REVEALED

The Berlin Wall separating Communist East Germany and democratic West Germany was raised in the early 1960s, a symbol of the Cold War. After the wall came down in 1989, uniting the two Germanys, Communism in Eastern Europe and the Soviet Union soon collapsed. The Soviet Union was dissolved in 1991 and became Russia and other republics, and the Iron Curtain that had isolated that part of the world was lifted. Free elections began ousting Communist governments across Eastern Europe. In the new spirit of openness, during the 1990s, the Russians released documents confirming that some American Communists did indeed spy for the Soviet Union. For the first time, researchers gained access to records of the Soviet secret police, the KGB, as well as records of the American Communist

Party that had been kept by the Soviets. The documents showed that espionage did occur during the Cold War.

More information about Americans spying for the Soviets was revealed when the National Security Agency, an independent agency in the Department of Defense responsible for intercepting and decoding foreign communications, released nearly 3,000 decryptions of early 1940s cables between Soviet operatives working in New York, San Francisco, and Washington, and their contacts in Moscow about a secret military operation known as the Venona Project. This was a joint effort of the United States and Great Britain to track Soviet intelligence during World War II. The records, opened to the public in 1995, revealed that the Soviet spy operation in America was extensive and relied on members and supporters of the American Communist Party. Spy cells had indeed operated in the State Department, the Treasury Department, and the Manhattan Project, which worked on developing the atomic bomb. Soviet agents included Alger Hiss and Julius Rosenberg, though it is still unclear what they did exactly and whether they ever actually endangered U.S. security or lives.

The majority of American Communists and sympathizers were not involved in any actual espionage, historians now say. Most did little more than support trade unions, read the *Daily Worker*, talk to each other about politics, and listen to folk music about immigrants, working people, and freedom. Also, not everyone agrees that the information on espionage that's been released in recent years is verifiable or accurate. As Victor Navasky, the editor of the *Nation*, writes, ". . . the debate about the domestic cold war—including what to call the repression that was part of it—tells us that while the cold war may be over, its ghosts linger on. And they continue to haunt."[2]

DISSENT IN A DEMOCRACY

The 1960 election of President John F. Kennedy, a politician who took a strong anti-Communist stance, showed that

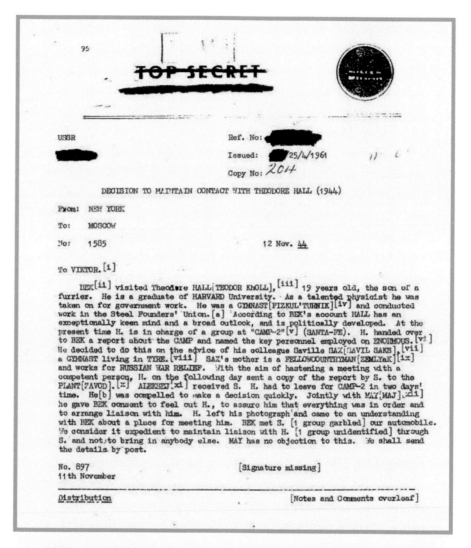

In 1995, the National Security Agency released documents from the Venona Project, a 1940s operation that intercepted messages from the Soviet Union to their spies in the United States. The documents revealed the extensive network of Soviet spies in America.

American voters still feared Communism. Even as they pushed for new social programs and civil rights legislation during the ensuing decade, many mainstream liberals joined McCarthyite conservatives to fight against Communism, including initial support of U.S. participation in the Vietnam War. Starting in the early 1960s and continuing through 1975, the United States sent aid and then soldiers to assist the government of South Vietnam in its war against Communist North Vietnam. Once again, Communism posed a deadly threat to American soldiers and national security.

Yet by the late 1960s, an explosive new political and social movement was raising the same questions that had faced the country during McCarthy's rise. The protestors filling the streets and college campuses questioned values that were the bedrock of American society but that they claimed had caused economic inequality, racism, pollution, and other problems. They turned against the Vietnam War. On rare occasions, the radical fringe of the protest movement resorted to violence. Many young people were challenging the status quo. They wanted to right what they perceived as wrongs. The FBI, still under its longtime director, J. Edgar Hoover, as well as the Central Intelligence Agency (CIA) and other federal agencies, tried to undermine the protestors, using controversial surveillance methods to stalk civil rights leaders and war protestors, among others. The Reverend Martin Luther King Jr. was one of many respected people investigated by the FBI. The FBI tried to prove he was influenced by the Communist Party because several of his associates had been former members. Historians now say the real intent was to derail the civil rights movement. After King's famous "I Have a Dream" speech on the steps of the Lincoln Memorial in 1963, FBI director Hoover called him the most dangerous black leader in the country and sought to increase surveillance on him and his associates. Attorney General Robert F. Kennedy gave permission for the FBI to wiretap his phones and hotel rooms. Thousands of FBI memos were written on King's activities. Once again, McCarthy era tactics were being employed.

Still the McCarthy generation was fading away. After leading the FBI since its founding nearly 50 years earlier, Hoover died while still at its helm in 1972. His last years were controversial. He faced rising criticism about his harassment of political dissenters and bypassing of conventional methods to gather evidence against people. Another figure of the Second Red Scare, Richard M. Nixon, was on his way down. Nixon had sat on the House Un-American Activities Committee and questioned Alger Hiss during the hearings in 1948. In his second term as U.S. president, in 1974, President Nixon found himself in the hot seat. Congress was investigating him for his involvement in the attempted wiretapping of the Democratic National Committee offices at the Watergate Hotel in Washington, D.C., during his 1972 reelection campaign. In 1974, Congress found Nixon guilty of obstructing justice and impeached him. Nixon resigned from the presidency on August 8, 1974. The techniques that may have worked decades earlier to smear political enemies were no longer acceptable.

AFTER 9/11

Terrorist attacks on American soil spawned a new era of anxiety in 2001. Once again, the balance between protecting national security and preserving personal freedoms was at risk. The tragic events of September 11, 2001, led to an outbreak of suspicion about so-called outsiders and dissenters, particularly Muslims and those of Arab descent. The airplanes that crashed into the World Trade Center in New York City and the Pentagon outside Washington, D.C., were piloted by terrorists who were Muslim and affiliated with al Qaeda, global terrorist organization. Fears arose about whether Muslims living in the United States or traveling by plane into the country were also potential threats.

Frequent terror warnings in the news, armed soldiers patrolling city streets, advice to families to stock up on emergency provisions, and warnings to look out for terrorists in the subways and airports all led to a state of high anxiety. Some people believed strong steps were needed to protect Americans, even if that meant bypassing basic civil rights and liberties ensured by law. Others disagreed, concerned that abridging fundamental rights to privacy or free speech might imperil the country as much as terrorism. "Will the task of fighting faceless global terrorists so expand the powers of the new security state that fundamental American freedoms are threatened—or lost?"[3] asks historian Haynes Johnson in *The Age of Anxiety: From McCarthyism to Terrorism.*

CIVIL LIBERTIES DURING CRISIS

The American Civil Liberties Union (ACLU) was founded in 1920 with the mission of defending and preserving the individual rights and liberties guaranteed by the Bill of Rights and the Constitution. One of its first efforts was to defend Communists and foreigners during the Palmer Raids after World War I. In 1925, the ACLU hired attorney Clarence Darrow to defend biology teacher John Scopes, accused of violating the Tennessee ban on teaching evolution.

The nonprofit group, with no political affiliation, is determined to protect the rights of all citizens, no matter how unpopular. Sometimes that stance has led to controversy, as in the late 1970s, when the ACLU defended the rights of neo-Nazis to display a swastika and march in Skokie, Illinois, a town with a 40 percent Jewish population. The U.S. Supreme Court in 1977 agreed with the ACLU, determining that the swastika is symbolic speech and protected by the First Amendment. Yet even the ACLU was swept up in the anti-Communist fervor in 1940, when the organization banned Communists and sympathizers from serving on its staff or committees.

After 9/11, the ACLU stepped up its vigilance, concerned that the civil liberties it had protected would be trampled on as the nation faced the very real threat of terrorism. In 2003, the ACLU

Shortly after 9/11, the USA PATRIOT Act was passed by Congress and signed by President George W. Bush in 2001. The controversial law gave the federal government and its law enforcement and intelligence-gathering agencies more powers to battle international and domestic terrorism. Yet critics worried that the law put civil liberties at risk. Wiretaps would not

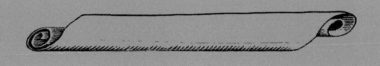

released a major report, "Freedom Under Fire: Dissent in Post-9/11 America." The following is the report's foreword, written by ACLU executive director Anthony D. Romero.

There is a pall over our country. In separate but related attempts to squelch dissent, the government has attacked the patriotism of its critics, police have barricaded and jailed protesters, and the New York Stock Exchange has revoked the press credentials of the most widely watched television network in the Arab world. A chilling message has gone out across America: Dissent if you must, but proceed at your own risk. . . .

Why should this disturb us? Because democracy is not a quiet business. Its lifeblood is the free and vibrant exchange of ideas. As *New York Times* columnist and author Thomas L. Friedman has pointed out, the war on terror is also a war of ideas. How are we going to convince holdouts in other countries about the importance of free speech and civil liberties if we show so little faith in our own?*

* Anthony D. Romero, foreword, "Freedom Under Fire: Dissent in Post-9/11 America." American Civil Liberties Union, May 8, 2003. http://www .aclu.org/national-security/freedom-under-fire-dissent-post-911-america.

need the same oversight by the courts. Police would have easier access to records of organizations and businesses, and the definition of providing support to terrorists was expanded.

One particular section, Section 215, raised a lot of questions. Section 215 allowed the federal government to obtain a court order to compel any business, organization, group, or library to release its records regarding any client. Thus, the book choices of patrons at public libraries were no longer private, but were accessible to the FBI. The American Library Association strongly protested this provision. Libraries in some cities posted signs to warn people that records of the materials they view and borrow could be accessed by the FBI. Some libraries even shredded records to protect the privacy of patrons. Yet those who supported the PATRIOT Act believed such measures were critical to protecting a nation at risk. When the Bush administration attempted to expand the PATRIOT Act two years later, in 2003, there was much opposition. Nevertheless, in 2006, Congress reauthorized the PATRIOT Act, keeping it mostly intact.

CAN THE RED SCARE RETURN?

By the 2000s, Communism no longer posed a national threat, as it had during the Cold War. Russia and China had become trading partners with the United States, though relations with both countries were evolving and sometimes tense. Despite the vast changes in world politics, the labels of "Communist" and "Socialist" were still being used to smear people. During the presidential campaign of Barack Obama in 2008, some opponents accused him of being a Socialist or a Communist. After he took office, during the heated debates over health care reform in 2009, similar charges were raised on cable news shows and conservative talk radio.

In September 2009, the *Wall Street Journal* published an editorial titled "The Red Scare Returns: The Right Dredges up a Familiar Bogeyman." In the editorial, Thomas Frank writes,

U.S. attorney Jim Letten defends the USA PATRIOT Act, a law passed after 9/11 that granted the federal government, law enforcement, and intelligence agencies broader guidelines in which to gather information on private individuals, organizations, and businesses.

"Can people really be moved to worry about communism with the Soviet Union gone? Can you really hope to gin up a red scare without almost no reds? Sure you can. Because red scares are fun. It's somehow ennobling to believe that our leaders have secretly betrayed us; that beneath the placid, suit-and-tie surface lurks a hideous alien philosophy; that time is running out for our country; that we alone have figured it out and now we are stepping bravely forward to give the congressman a piece of our minds."[4] To be sure, the label of "Communist" no longer carries the same charge that it once did. Nevertheless, it's still being used to tar someone with opposing political views, with little regard to truth or facts.

BLACKLISTERS' CREDITS

Though over a half century has passed, those caught in the web of the Second Red Scare haven't forgotten. Some are still trying to get back some of what they lost. Starting in the 1980s, the Writers Guild of America, which represents writers in the motion picture, broadcast, and related industries, began restoring the credits of Hollywood professionals who'd been blacklisted for refusing to testify before the House Un-American Activities Committee. Some of them had continued to work but could not use their real names. Nor were they paid their usual wages. As a consequence, the names of writers were left off the screen credits of dozens of films. Instead, pseudonyms were used, or other people were given credit. The Writers Guild has helped document and restore accurate credits to dozens of films. The group has also recommended that the companies owning the films change the credits in video releases and prints in the future.

Among those whose names have been restored is Michael Wilson, one of the finest screenplay writers in Hollywood history. As a college student during the Great Depression, Wilson had joined the Communist Party. He later became a busy writer in Hollywood. In 1952, Wilson won an Academy Award for cowriting an adapted screenplay for *A Place in the Sun*. After he refused to testify before HUAC, he was blacklisted and was unable to work in Hollywood. He moved to France, where he worked on the screenplays of three classics—*Friendly Persuasion* (1956), *The Bridge on the River Kwai* (1957), and early drafts of *Lawrence of Arabia* (1962). He was paid little, and his name was on none of the films' credits.

In a special Academy Award ceremony in 1985, Wilson and another exiled writer, Carl Foreman, were finally given the Oscar that they had earned for *The Bridge on the River Kwai*. In 1995, Wilson's name was restored to the credits of *Lawrence of Arabia*. His name is also now listed on DVDs of *Friendly Persuasion*. Wilson died in 1978, so he did not live to see his credits restored. At the awards ceremony in 1995, Wilson's wife, Zelma, read a statement that he had written earlier about the McCarthy era:

> I fear that unless you remember this dark epoch and under-
> stand it, you may be doomed to replay it—not with the
> same cast of characters, of course, or on the same issues.
> But I foresee a day coming in your lifetime, if not in mine,
> when a new crisis of belief will grip this republic; when
> diversity of opinion will be labeled disloyalty; when chill-
> ing decisions affecting our culture will be made in the
> boardrooms of conglomerates and networks. If this gloomy
> scenario should come to pass, I trust that you younger men
> and women will shelter the mavericks and dissenters in
> your ranks and protect their right to work. The Guild will
> have need of rebels and heretics if it is to survive as a union
> of free writers. The nation will have need of them if it is to
> survive as an open society.[5]

Former blacklist victims are also working to protect others from the fates that they had to endure. In 2009, a group of
people who had been on the blacklists filed a brief in support
of a case before the Supreme Court, *Holder v. Humanitarian
Law Project.* In the case, a set of human rights groups and other
supporters challenged the constitutionality of the material
support statute, a law that criminalizes support or assistance,
including aid, political advocacy, and literature distribution, to
any foreign group that the government has designated a terrorist group. Critics of the statute say that groups that do not agree
with U.S. foreign policy are sometimes wrongly branded as terrorist, and that the statute criminalizes what have always been
constitutionally protected activities. Supporters of the statute
disagree, maintaining that in a world where terrorist activities
cross national borders, the United States must do what it can
to protect its citizens. One of the former blacklist victims who

signed the brief is Irwin Corey, a comedian and satirist. "We lived and suffered through a time when repression for one's political ideas was all too widely accepted and practiced. We file this brief in hopes that Americans do not repeat that history,"[6] he said.

APOLOGY ACCEPTED

In 1989, playwright Arthur Miller reflected on his play *The Crucible*, which by then had become standard reading in high schools and was staged frequently around the world. He said that the play about the seventeenth-century witch hunts in Salem, Massachusetts, was not just inspired by the McCarthy era, but also by other times when people were afraid to speak out and, instead, latched onto a popular tide. "I have wondered if one of the reasons the play continues like this is its symbolic unleashing of the specter of order's fragility," he wrote. "When certainties evaporate with each dawn, the unknowable is always around the corner. We know how much depends on mere trust and good faith and a certain respect for the human person, and how easily breached these are. And we know as well how close to the edge we live and how weak we really are and how quickly swept by fear the mass of us can become when our panic button is pushed. It is also, I suppose, that the play reaffirms the ultimate power of courage and clarity of mind whose ultimate fruit is liberty."[7] Miller died in 2005.

In February 2009, the San Diego school district invited folk singer Pete Seeger to perform a concert. The invitation was extended not just because Seeger was a world-famous musician. Rather, the San Diego School Board was trying to right what it deemed a wrong, one that had occurred nearly 50 years earlier. At that time, in May 1960, San Diego had asked Seeger to either sign an oath against Communism or not play a concert planned at Hoover High School's auditorium. Seeger refused to sign the oath, and a judge allowed the concert to proceed, but the shadow of the past still loomed large.

The school board passed a referendum, declaring that it "deeply regrets its predecessors' actions" and offered an apology to one of "our dearest national treasures."[8] Seeger, by then 89 years old, called the referendum "a measure of justice that our right to freedom of expression has been vindicated."[9] The school board had been pressured not to allow the concert by the anti-Communist American Legion in San Diego. "I was used to things like this, way back in what I called the Frightened '50s. They were dangerous times,"[10] Seeger told a local newspaper. One school board member had seen Seeger and rocker Bruce Springsteen singing "This Land Is Your Land," a song written by Woody Guthrie, at President Barack Obama's presidential inauguration at the Lincoln Memorial in January 2009. Of her decision to write the apology resolution, school board member Katherine Nakamura said, "It just seemed to me to be the right thing to do."[11]

CHRONOLOGY

1908   Joseph R. McCarthy is born in Wisconsin on November 14.

1939   Hatch Act makes membership in Communist Party an obstacle to federal employment.

1940   Smith Act makes it a criminal offense for a person to advocate the overthrow of the government.

1941   The U.S. enters World War II. Fighting continues until 1945.

TIMELINE

1908
Joseph R. McCarthy is born on a farm in Wisconsin on November 14.

1947
The Hollywood Ten are blacklisted by the film industry after refusing to testify before the House Un-American Activities Committee.

1908 ——————— 1950

1946
McCarthy is elected to the U.S. Senate.

1950
The McCarran Act bans Communist organizations and excludes aliens and subversives from entering the country or becoming citizens; McCarthy accuses the State Department of employing Communists.

1942 U.S. Department of Justice starts a list of organizations suspected of subversion.

1945 The House Un-American Activities Committee (HUAC) succeeds the Special Committee to Investigate Un-American Activities, created in 1938.

1947 McCarthy takes office as Republican senator from Wisconsin.

The House Un-American Activities Committee investigates Communism in Hollywood.

President Truman issues Executive Order 9835 to search out disloyal persons in the U.S. government.

1953
Julius and Ethel Rosenberg are executed for espionage; Arthur Miller's play *The Crucible* premieres in New York.

1957
McCarthy dies of liver disease on May 2.

1953   **2008**

1954
During the Army-McCarthy hearings, Edward R. Murrow's program *See It Now* helps turn public opinion against McCarthy; The Senate, on a vote of 67 to 22, censures McCarthy.

2008
New information shows that Julius Rosenberg and Alger Hiss were most likely Soviet spies.

1949	Soviets test an atom bomb; Mao Tse-tung declares China a Communist republic.
1950	McCarthy's Lincoln Day speech on February 9 raises fears of Communists in the State Department.
	McCarran Act bans Communist organizations and excludes aliens and subversives from entering the country or becoming citizens.
	Former State Department lawyer Alger Hiss is convicted of perjury.
1950–1953	United States fights in the Korean War.
1953	Julius and Ethel Rosenberg, convicted of espionage, are executed at Sing Sing prison.
	President Dwight Eisenhower takes office.
1954	McCarthy accuses the U.S. Army of Communist infiltration during the televised Army-McCarthy hearings.
	Edward R. Murrow attacks McCarthy on *See It Now*'s "A Report on Senator Joseph R. McCarthy" on March 9.
	U.S. Senate issues a condemnation of McCarthy for two counts of conduct unbecoming a senator on December 2.
1956	J. Edgar Hoover starts COINTELPRO to undermine political dissidents.
1957	On May 2, McCarthy dies of liver disease at the age of 48.
2008	New information shows that Julius Rosenberg and Alger Hiss were most likely spies.

NOTES

CHAPTER 1

1. Joseph Loftus, "Arthur Miller and Dr. Nathan Indicted on Contempt Charges," *New York Times*, February 19, 1957. http://www.nytimes.com/books/00/11/12/specials/miller-indicted.html?scp=1&sq=Arthur%20Miller%20and%20Dr.%20Nathan%20Indicted%20on%20Contempt%20Charges%20&st=cse.

2. C.P. Trussell, "Elia Kazan Admits He Was Red in 30's," *New York Times*, April 13, 1952. http://select.nytimes.com/mem/archive/pdf?res=F60D15FE3C5E177B93C0A8178FD85F468585F9.

3. Arthur Miller, "Again They Drink from the Cup of Suspicion," *New York Times*, November 26, 1989. http://partners.nytimes.com/books/00/11/12/specials/miller-drink.html.

4. Arthur Miller, "Why Elia Should Get His Oscar," *Guardian*, March 6, 1999. http://www.guardian.co.uk/culture/1999/mar/06/awardsandprizes.

5. "Elia Kazan," *American Masters*, PBS. http://www.pbs.org/wnet/americanmasters/episodes/elia-kazan/about-elia-kazan/642/.

CHAPTER 2

1. A. Mitchell Palmer, "The Case Against the Red," *Forum* 63(1920): pp. 173–185. http://chnm.gmu.edu/courses/hist409/palmer.html.

2. Ellen Schrecker, *Many Are the Crimes: McCarthyism in America.* Boston: Little Brown & Co., 1998, p. 4.

3. Allan L. Damon, "The Great Red Scare," *American Heritage Magazine*, February 1968. http://www.americanheritage.com/articles/magazine/ah/1968/2/1968_2_22.shtml.

4. Schrecker, *Many Are the Crimes*, p. 60.

5. *Schenck v. United States*, Supreme Court Collection, Cornell University Law School. http://www.law.cornell.edu/supct/html/historics/USSC_CR_0249_0047_ZO.

6. Franklin D. Roosevelt, "Statement on the Sit-Down Strikes in Michigan," October 25, 1938, The American Presidents Project. http://www.presidency.ucsb.edu/ws/index.php?pid=15555.

7. Schrecker, *Many Are the Crimes*, p. 92.

8. Kenneth D. Ackerman, *Young J. Edgar Hoover, The Red Scare, and the Assault on Civil Liberties.* New York: Carroll & Graf, 2007, p. 406.

CHAPTER 3

1. Schrecker, *Many Are the Crimes*, p. 317.

2. Ted Morgan, *Reds: McCarthyism in Twentieth-Century America.* New York: Random House, 2003, p. 517.

3. Ronald Reagan Testimony Before HUAC, 1947. http:// wps.prenhall.com/wps/media/ objects/108/110880/ch26_a5_ d1.pdf.

4. Schrecker, *Many Are the Crimes*, p. 321.

5. Ibid., p. 330.

6. Albert Fried, *McCarthyism: The Great American Red Scare. A Documentary History*. New York: Oxford University Press, 1997, p. 46.

7. Ibid., p. 160.

8. *Adler v. Board of Education of the City of New York*, Supreme Court Collection, Cornell University Law School. http://www4.law .cornell.edu/supct/html/historics/ USSC_CR_0342_0485_ZO.html.

9. Ibid.

10. Fried, *McCarthyism*, p. 20.

CHAPTER 4

1. Morgan, *Reds*, pp. 384–385.

2. Ibid., p. 385.

3. Arthur Herman, *Joseph McCarthy: Reexamining the Life and Legacy of America's Most Hated Senator*. New York: The Free Press, 2000, p. 101.

4. Fried, *McCarthyism*, p. 126.

5. Ibid., p. 128.

6. Ibid.

7. David Oshinsky, *A Conspiracy So Immense: The World of Joe McCarthy*. New York: Oxford University Press, 2005, p. 164.

8. Ibid., p. 165.

9. Morgan, *Reds*, p. 410.

10. Ibid., p. 412.

11. Ibid.

12. "Congress Weighed in the Balance," *Time*, October 22, 1951. http://www.time.com/ time/magazine/article/ 0,9171,815585,00.html.

13. "Address at the Dedication of the New Washington Headquarters of the American Legion," August 14, 1951, Harry S. Truman Library and Museum. http://www.trumanlibrary.org/ publicpapers/index.php?pid= 406&st=&st1= .

CHAPTER 5

1. Ronald Radosh and Joyce Milton, *The Rosenberg File: A Search for the Truth*. New York: Holt, Rinehart and Winston, 1983, p. 172.

2. Ibid., p. 173.

3. Ibid., pp. 267–268.

4. Ibid., p. 269.

5. Ibid., p. 284.

6. William R. Conklin, "Atom Spy Couple Sentenced to Die; Aide Gets 30 Years," *New York Times*, April 6, 1961. http://select .nytimes.com/mem/archive/pdf? res=F60C1FF9355A1A7B93C4A 9178FD85F458585F9.

7. Kenneth D. Ackerman, *Young J. Edgar Hoover, the Red Scare, and the Assault on Civil Liberties*. New York: Carroll & Graf, 2007, p. 407.

8. "False Testimony Clinched Rosenberg Spy Trial," BBC News, December 6, 2001. http:// news.bbc.co.uk/2/hi/americas/ 1695240.stm.

9. Ibid.

10. "Robert Meeropol: Fighting the Frame-up from the Rosenbergs to Mumia," *Revolutionary Worker*, #122, September 19, 1999.

http://rwor.org/a/v21/1020-029/
1022/meero.htm.

11. Herman, *Joseph McCarthy*,
p. 194.

CHAPTER 6

1. Herman, *Joseph McCarthy*, p. 261.
2. Executive Sessions of the Senate
Permanent Subcommittee on
Investigations of the Committee
on Government Operations,
Vol. 2, 83rd Congress, 1953,
p. 946. http://www.senate.gov/
artandhistory/history/resources/
pdf/Volume2.pdf.
3. Oshinsky, *A Conspiracy So
Immense*, p. 271.
4. Tom Wicker, *Shooting Star: The
Brief Arc of Joe McCarthy*. Orlando: Harcourt Inc., 2006, p. 151.
5. "Investigations: One Man's
Army," *Time*, March 1, 1954.
http://www.time.com/time/
magazine/article/0,9171,819478-
2,00.html#ixzz0YGOnINOY.
6. Herman, *Joseph McCarthy*,
pp. 250–251.
7. Fried, *McCarthyism*, p. 186.
8. Ibid, p. 187.
9. Richard M. Fried, *Nightmare
in Red: The McCarthy Era in
Perspective*. Oxford U.K.: Oxford
University Press, 1990, p. 140.
10. "National Affairs: For Joe:
Phoeey!" *Time*, April 19, 1954.
http://www.time.com/time/
magazine/article/0,9171,860528-
2,00.html.
11. "'I Have Sung for Hobos, I Have
Sung for the Rockefellers.' Pete
Seeger Refuses to 'Sing' for the
HUAC," *History Matters*. http://
historymatters.gmu.edu/d/6457.
12. Ibid.

CHAPTER 7

1. Herman, *Joseph McCarthy*,
p. 276.
2. Ibid., p. 277.
3. "The Vice-Presidency: How to
Shoot Rats," *Time*, March 22,
1954. http://www.time.com/
time/magazine/article/0,9171,
819558-1,00.html.
4. Wicker, *Shooting Star*, p. 151.
5. Albert Fried, *McCarthyism*,
pp. 188–189.
6. Ibid., p. 190.
7. Ibid.
8. "Transcript of Senate Resolution
301: Censure of Senator Joseph
McCarthy (1954)," *Our Documents: 100 Milestone
Documents from the National
Archives*. http://www.our
documents.gov/doc.php?doc=
86&page=transcript.
9. "The Congress: The Censure of
Joe McCarthy," *Time*, October 4,
1954. http://www.time.com/
time/magazine/article/0,9171,
857533-7,00.html.
10. Jean Edwards Smith, "How to
End a War Eisenhower's Way,"
New York Times, April 11, 2009.
http://100days.blogs.nytimes
.com/2009/04/11/how-to-end-
a-war-eisenhowers-way/.
11. Ibid.
12. Harry Schwartz, "Reds Renounced by Howard Fast," *New
York Times*, February 1, 1957.
http://select.nytimes.com/mem/
archive/pdf?res=F50910FA3D5F1
47B93C3A91789D85F438585F9.
13. Albert Fried, *McCarthyism*,
p. 192.
14. *Watkins v. United States*, Supreme
Court Cases, Cornell University

Law School. http://www.law
.cornell.edu/supct/html/historics/
USSC_CR_0354_0178_ZO.html.

15. Richard M. Fried, *Nightmare in
Red*, p. 92.

16. "COINTELPRO: The FBI's
Covert Action Programs Against
American Citizens: Final Report
of the Select Committee to
Investigate Governmental
Operations." http://www.icdc
.com/~paulwolf/cointelpro/
churchfinalreportIIIa.htm.

17. Ibid.

18. Richard M. Fried, *Nightmare in
Red*, p. 195.

CHAPTER 8

1. Oshinsky, *A Conspiracy So
Immense*, p. 507.

2. Victor Navasky, "Cold War
Ghosts," *Nation*, June 28, 2001.
http://www.thenation.com/doc/
20010716/navasky/1.

3. Haynes Johnson, *The Age of
Anxiety: McCarthyism to Terror-
ism.* Orlando: Houghton Mifflin
Harcourt, 2005, p. 5.

4. Thomas Frank, "The Red Scare
Returns: The Right Dredges
Up a Familiar Bogeyman," *Wall
Street Journal*, September 9, 2009.
http://online.wsj.com/article/SB1
0001424052970203440104574401
163387229496.html.

5. Joseph Dmohowski, "Under the
Table: Michael Wilson and the
Screenplay for *The Bridge on the
River Kwai*," *Cineaste*, March 22,
2009. http://www.thefreelibrary
.com/%22Under+the+table%22:
+Michael+Wilson+and+the+
Screenplay+for+The+Bridge...-
a0195135109.

6. "McCarthy Era Blacklist Victims,
Peace Groups, Academics, and
Media File Amicus Briefs in CCR
Case," Center for Constitutional
Rights. http://ccrjustice.org/
newsroom/press-releases/
mccarthy-era-blacklist-victims%
2C-peace-groups%2C-academics
%2C-and-media-file-amic.

7. Arthur Miller, "Again They Drink
from the Cup of Suspicion," *New
York Times*, November 26, 1989.
http://partners.nytimes.com/
books/00/11/12/specials/miller-
drink.html.

8. "School Board Offers Apology
to Singer Pete Seeger," *Times-
Herald Record*, February 11,
2009. http://www.record
online.com/apps/pbcs.dll/
article?AID=/20090211/
ENTERTAIN/90211017/-1/
ENTERTAIN37.

9. Ibid.

10. Ibid.

11. Ibid.

BIBLIOGRAPHY

Ackerman, Kenneth D. *Young J. Edgar Hoover: The Red Scare, and the Assault on Civil Liberties.* New York: Carroll & Graf, 2007.

Adler v. Board of Education of the City of New York, Supreme Court Collection, Cornell University Law School. http://www4.law.cornell.edu/supct/html/historics/USSC_CR_0342_0485_ZO.html.

Blumenthal, Ralph. "When Suspicion of Teachers Ran Unchecked," *New York Times,* June 15, 2009. http://www.nytimes.com/2009/06/16/nyregion/16teachers.html?pagewanted=2&_r=1&ref=nyregion.

Christensen, Jen. "FBI Tracked King's Every Move," CNN, December 29, 2008. http://www.cnn.com/2008/US/03/31/mlk.fbi.conspiracy/index.html.

Conklin, William R. "Atom Spy Couple Sentenced to Die; Aide Gets 30 Years," *New York Times,* April 6, 1961. http://select.nytimes.com/mem/archive/pdf?res=F60C1FF9355A1A7B93C4A9178FD85F458585F9.

Damon, Allan L. "The Great Red Scare," *American Heritage Magazine,* February 1968. http://www.americanheritage.com/articles/magazine/ah/1968/2/1968_2_22.shtml.

Dmohowski, Joseph. "Under the Table: Michael Wilson and the Screenplay for *The Bridge on the River Kwai," Cineaste,* March 22, 2009. http://www.thefreelibrary.com/%22Under+the+table%22:+Michael+Wilson+and+the+Screenplay+for+The+Bridge...-a0195135109.

Dubord, Steven J. "Librarians Unite Against Patriot Act Provisions," *New American,* December 4, 2009. http://www

.thenewamerican.com/index.php/usnews/congress/2467-librarians-unite-against-patriot-act-provisions.

"Edward R. Murrow's Report from Buchenwald," Jewish Virtual Library. http://www.jewishvirtuallibrary.org/jsource/Holocaust/murrow.html.

Edwards, Bob. *Edward R. Murrow and the Birth of Broadcast Journalism.* New York: John Wiley & Sons, Inc., 2004.

"Elia Kazan," *American Masters,* PBS. http://www.pbs.org/wnet/americanmasters/episodes/elia-kazan/about-elia-kazan/642/.

Executive Sessions of the Senate Permanent Subcommittee on Investigations of the Committee on Government Operations, Vol. 2, 83rd Congress, 1953. http://www.senate.gov/artand history/history/resources/pdf/Volume2.pdf

"False Testimony Clinched Rosenberg Spy Trial," BBC News, December 6, 2001. http://news.bbc.co.uk/2/hi/americas/1695240.stm.

Fariello, Griffin. *Red Scare: Memories of the American Inquisition, an Oral History.* New York: Norton, 1995.

Frank, Thomas. "The Red Scare Returns: The Right Dredges Up a Familiar Bogeyman," *Wall Street Journal,* September 9, 2009. http://online.wsj.com/article/SB1000142405297020344010457440116338722 9496.html.

Fried, Albert. *McCarthyism: The Great American Red Scare. A Documentary History.* New York: Oxford University Press, 1997.

Fried, Richard M. *Nightmare in Red: The McCarthy Era in Perspective.* Oxford, U.K.: Oxford University Press, 1990.

"Herblock's History: Political Cartoons from the Crash to the Millennium," Library of Congress. http://www.loc.gov/rr/print/swann/herblock/fire.html.

Herman, Arthur. *Joseph McCarthy: Reexamining the Life and Legacy of America's Most Hated Senator.* New York: Free Press, 2000.

"Investigations: One Man's Army," *Time*, March 1, 1954. http://www.time.com/time/magazine/article/0,9171,819478-1,00.html.

Johnson, Haynes. *The Age of Anxiety: McCarthyism to Terrorism.* Orlando: Houghton Mifflin Harcourt, 2006.

Loftus, Joseph. "Arthur Miller and Dr. Nathan Indicted on Contempt Charges," *New York Times*, February 19, 1957. http://www.nytimes.com/books/00/11/12/specials/miller-indicted.html?scp=1&sq=Arthur%20Miller%20and%20Dr.%20Nathan%20Indicted%20on%20Contempt%20Charges%20&st=cse.

"McCarthy Era Blacklist Victims, Peace Groups, Academics, and Media File Amicus Briefs in CCR Case," Center for Constitutional Rights. http://ccrjustice.org/newsroom/press-releases/mccarthy-era-blacklist-victims%2C-peace-groups%2C-academics%2C-and-media-file-amic.

Miller, Arthur. "Again They Drink from the Cup of Suspicion," *New York Times*, November 26, 1989. http://partners.nytimes.com/books/00/11/12/specials/miller-drink.html.

Miller, Arthur. "Why Elia Should Get His Oscar," *Guardian*, March 6, 1999. http://www.guardian.co.uk/culture/1999/mar/06/awardsandprizes.

Miller, Laura M. "The Testimony of Walter E. Disney Before the House Committee on Un-American Activities (24 October 1947)," *Dictionary of American History*. The Gale Group Inc., 2003. Encyclopedia.com. http://www.encyclopedia.com/doc/1G2-3401804827.html.

"National Affairs: Calm After Censure," *Time*, October 11, 1954. http://www.time.com/time/magazine/article/0,9171,936427,00.html.

Navasky, Victor. "Cold War Ghosts," *Nation*, June 28, 2001. http://www.thenation.com/doc/20010716/navasky/1.

Oshinsky, David M. *A Conspiracy So Immense: The World of Joe McCarthy*. New York: Oxford University Press, 2005.

"Robert Meeropol: Fighting the Frame-up from the Rosenbergs to Mumia," *Revolutionary Worker*, #122, September 19, 1999. http://rwor.org/a/v21/1020-029/1022/meero.htm.

Roberts, Sam. "Figure in Rosenberg Case Admits to Spying," *New York Times*, Sept. 11, 2008. http://www.nytimes.com/2008/09/12/nyregion/12spy.html?_r=1.

Robeson, Paul. *Here I Stand*. Boston: Beacon Press, 1971.

"Robeson Receives Posthumous Grammy." *New York Times*, February 25, 1998.

Romero, Anthony D. Foreword, "Freedom Under Fire: Dissent in Post-9/11 America," American Civil Liberties Union, May 8, 2003. http://www.aclu.org/national-security/freedom-under-fire-dissent-post-911-america.

"School Board Offers Apology to Singer Pete Seeger," *Times-Herald Record*, February 11, 2009. http://www.recordonline.com/apps/pbcs.dll/article?AID=/20090211/ENTERTAIN/90211017/-1/ENTERTAIN37.

Schrecker, Ellen. *Many Are the Crimes: McCarthyism in America*. Boston: Little, Brown, 1998.

Schwartz, Harry. "Reds Renounced by Howard Fast," *New York Times*, February 1, 1957. http://select.nytimes.com/mem/archive/pdf?res=F50910FA3D5F147B93C3A91789D85F438585F9.

Seeger, Pete. "'I Have Sung for Hobos, I Have Sung for the Rockefellers.' Pete Seeger Refuses to 'Sing' for the HUAC," History Matters. http://historymatters.gmu.edu/d/6457.

"The Senate: The Passing of McCarthy," *Time*, May 13, 1957. http://www.time.com/time/magazine/article/0,9171,867634-1,00.html.

Shogan, Robert. *No Sense of Decency: The Army-McCarthy Hearings: A Demagogue Falls and Television Takes Charge of American Politics*. Chicago: Ivan R. Dee, 2009.

"Transcript of Senate Resolution 301: Censure of Senator Joseph McCarthy (1954)," *Our Documents: 100 Milestone Documents from the National Archives*. http://www.ourdocuments.gov/doc.php?doc=86&page=transcript.

Trussell, C.P. "Elia Kazan Admits He Was Red in 30's," *New York Times*, April 13, 1952. http://select.nytimes.com/mem/archive/pdf?res=F60D15FE3C5E177B93C0A8178FD85F468585F9.

"The Vice-Presidency: How to Shoot Rats," *Time*, March 22, 1954. http://www.time.com/time/magazine/article/0,9171,819558-1,00.html.

Watkins v. United States, Supreme Court Cases, Cornell University Law School. http://www.law.cornell.edu/supct/html/historics/USSC_CR_0354_0178_ZO.html.

Weinraub, Bernard. "A McCarthy Era Memory That Can Still Chill." *New York Times*, January 16, 1997. http://www.nytimes.com/1997/01/16/movies/a-mccarthy-era-memory-that-can-still-chill.html.

Wicker, Tom. *Shooting Star: The Brief Arc of Joe McCarthy*. Orlando: Harcourt Inc., 2006.

FURTHER READING

Barson, Michael, and Steven Heller. *Red Scared! The Commie Menace in Propaganda and Pop Culture*. San Francisco: Chronicle Books, 2000.

Burnett, Betty. *The Trial of Julius and Ethel Rosenberg: A Primary Source Account*. New York: Rosen Publishing Group, 2004.

Cushman, Karen. *The Loud Silence of Francine Green*. San Francisco: Clarion Books, 2006.

Fariello, Griffin. *Red Scare: Memories of the American Inquisition, an Oral History*. New York: Norton, 1995.

Fried, Albert. *McCarthyism: The Great American Red Scare: A Documentary History*. New York: Oxford University Press, 1997.

Klingaman, William K. *Encyclopedia of the McCarthy Era*. New York: Facts On File, Inc., 1996.

Levine, Ellen. *Catch a Tiger by the Toe*. New York: Viking, 2005.

Ritchie, Nigel, *Communism: Ideas of the Modern World*. Austin: Raintree Steck-Vaughn Publishers, 2001.

Robeson, Paul. *Here I Stand*. Boston: Beacon Press, 1988.

Schrecker, Ellen, ed. *The Age of McCarthyism: A Brief History with Documents*. Boston: St. Martin's, 1994.

Wicker, Tom. *Shooting Star: The Brief Arc of Joe McCarthy*. Orlando: Harcourt Inc., 2006.

WEB SITES
The All Powers Project
http://www.lib.washington.edu/EXHIBITS/ALLPOWERS/film.html
A list of films that played a role in the Red Scare.

Arthur Miller

http://www.neh.gov/whoweare/miller/biography.html

A look at the life and works of Arthur Miller.

The Robeson Foundation

http://www.paulrobesonfoundation.org/galleryintro.html

A look at Paul Robeson's life and career, with photographs.

The Rosenberg Fund for Children

http://www.rfc.org/

A nonprofit family foundation that provides assistance to children of parents targeted for political activism and provides information about the Rosenberg trial and family.

Tracked in America

http://www.trackedinamerica.org/

Oral histories and first-hand stories of the McCarthy era and other times in American history where people have been targeted for unpopular views.

MOVIES
Salt of the Earth (1954)

Created by a group of blacklisted Hollywood film workers, this is the story of a New Mexico mining strike.

The Front (1976)

Woody Allen tells the story of the Red Scare in a film that features many blacklisted victims who lost their careers.

The Way We Were (1973)

A romantic comedy starring Robert Redford and Barbara Streisand about a couple who weathered the Red Scare from the 1930s to the 1960s.

Good Night, and Good Luck (2005)

This fact-based drama chronicles television broadcaster Edward R. Murrow's exposé of Senator Joe McCarthy during the Army-McCarthy hearings in 1954.

PHOTO CREDITS

INDEX

About the Author

ANN MALASPINA has written many books for young people, including *The Underground Railroad: The Journey to Freedom* (Chelsea House, 2010). She began her career as a newspaper reporter in Boston. As she researched the McCarthy era, she was curious about how journalists did their jobs in a time when dissent was often seen as unpatriotic. She found that many, such as broadcast journalist Edward R. Murrow and newspaper columnist Drew Pearson, took great risks to report honestly on what they saw and heard. The work of these journalists and others helped to keep the public informed during those tumultuous years and provided a vital historical record for future generations. Ann likes to read newspapers with her family in northern New Jersey.